an avalanche of anoraks

an
avalanche
of
anoraks

Robert J. White

Crown Trade Paperbacks, New York

Published by Crown Trade Paperbacks, 201 East 50th Street, New York,
New York 10022. Member of the Crown Publishing Group.

Random House, Inc. New York, Toronto, London, Sydney, Auckland

CROWN TRADE PAPERBACKS and colophon are trademarks of Crown
Publishers, Inc.

Manufactured in the United States of America

Design by Lauren Dong

Library of Congress Cataloging-in-Publication Data
White, Robert J., 1939–
    An avalanche of anoraks / Robert J. White — 1st ed.
       p.   cm.
    1. English language—Foreign words and phrases—Dictionaries.
    2. English language—Etymology—Dictionaries. I. Title.
    PE1582.A3W48   1994
    422'.4'03—dc20
    94-9851
    CIP

ISBN 0-517-88131-4

10 9 8 7 6 5 4 3 2 1

First Edition

To My Wife,
Jane Giegengack White

contents

acknowledgments

I wish to thank Ellen Cavolina; Beverly and David Crofoot; Professor Tamara M. Green, chairman of the Department of Classical and Oriental Studies of Hunter College; Professor Eckhard Kuhn-Osius of the German Department of Hunter College; and Dianne Tkach and the staff of the Tuckahoe (N.Y.) Public Library for their kind help in the preparation of this book—be it in the form of encouragement, enthusiasm, or actual information on loan-words from other languages.

My grateful thanks are also due to Lucie D. Giegengack, whose abiding love of words and delight in etymological trivia has always been an inspiration.

I am especially indebted to Jane Cavolina, my brilliant and tireless editor, for her insightful suggestions and painstaking editing of every page; to my children, Elizabeth, David, and Nancy, for their patience, love and support; and, finally, to my extraordinary wife, Jane, to whom this book is dedicated.

introduction

For more than a thousand years, the English language has borrowed promiscuously from virtually every other language spoken on this planet. In fact, a few words can be said to have entered our language even before English existed as a language. For example, one of the oldest borrowed words in English is the word **mile,** which was the shortened form of the Latin **milia pasuum,** or "thousands of paces."

In 55 B.C., the great military genius Julius Caesar invaded Britain. Less than a century later, the Roman emperor Claudius dispatched an expeditionary force against the island. Within forty years, the Romans had advanced as far north as Scotland. The people of Britain at this time spoke a Celtic tongue. Latin, the official language of the Roman occupation, had little effect on the Celtic of the natives. They did, however, adopt a few useful words, **mile** for one. Four hundred years later, when Germanic-speaking tribes—Angles, Saxons, and Jutes—began their great incursions into Britain, they wiped out, to a great extent, the native Celtic of the Britons but, in the process, picked up a few of the Latin words that the Celts had previously borrowed from the Romans—the word **mile** among them.

Since that time, English has been a persistent borrower of words from the languages of those with whom it has come into contact—whether through trade, cultural intercourse, or even war. The expression the **boondocks,** for example, signifying "an uninhabited area with thick natural vegetation," came into English from Tagalog, the native language of the Philippines, as recently as sixty years ago. Whereas the word means "mountain" to the people of the Philippines, American soldiers used the word to describe any kind of rough back country, any out-of-the-way locale.

The word **boondocks** first came to the attention of the American public during an investigation into the brutal methods of training employed by Marines at Camp Lejeune in North Carolina. According to the official records, recruits were regularly subjected to forced night marches "into the boondocks," which now included some low-lying swampy areas where at least one recruit drowned. The investigation ended, but the word remained. Its infamous history all but forgotten, the word **boondocks** is now synonymous with any remote rural area distant from the excitement of big cities or large towns, a word roughly equivalent to "the sticks."

From Italian, we have borrowed such geological terms as **volcano** and **lava;** such musical terms as **soprano, opera, concerto, piano,** and **libretto;** and a few names for vegetables, including **zucchini** and **broccoli.**

Our word **macaroni,** which also comes from Italian, has a long and fascinating history. The Italians (via the Romans) borrowed the Greek word **makaria,** meaning "blessed," which was used to describe a sacrificial cake made out of a mixture of broth and barley. For the Italians, then, the word signified any jumbled-up mixture, because macaroni was served with different sauces. Once taken into English, besides meaning "pasta in the form of dried, hollow tubes" served with different sauces, the word also came to mean a dandy or a fop, one who affected Continental mannerisms. This is the meaning in "Yankee Doodle Dandy," a mocking song sung by British soldiers to make fun of the poorly dressed colonists. There was, incidentally, a militia from Maryland during the Revolutionary War who were known as the Macaronies because they wore splendid uniforms otherwise unknown in the colonies.

Every year, as families gather round the table for Thanksgiving and as hot plates are carefully being consigned to maple or mahogany credenzas, it is comforting to realize how much meals have changed since the Renaissance of the Borgias, when the Italians first coined the word. A **credenza,** derived from the Latin word **credere,** "to believe, to trust," was originally a side table where food was tasted for poison before serving. If the food passed the **credenza,** you could **trust** it and **believe** that it was safe to eat.

It is no less reassuring to know during the flu season that the Italian scientists who named the disease **influenza** believed that different planets controlled certain throat and bronchial diseases, and that the unpredictability of outbreaks of the flu was due to the influence, the **influenza,** of the planets.

Arabic has given us **zenith** and **nadir, zero,** and **algebra.** It has given us several other **al-** words as well, such as **alcohol, albatross, alchemy, alfalfa,** and **alcove.** Not to mention a **sofa** to sit in, a **sash** for our shoulders or waist, and **caraway** seeds for our rye bread.

India, whether through Hindi or Sanskrit, has lent us **pajamas, pun-**

dit, **jungle,** and **shampoo** (which, in Hindi, means "to knead bread"). It was home, too, to the first **thug,** which originally referred to worshipers of the Hindu goddess Kali, who ambushed unsuspecting victims, stole their valuables, and, more often than not, cut their throats.

India has also supplied the words **chintz, dinghy,** and **dungarees.**

The word **dungarees** may come from India, but the words **jeans** and **denim** come from France, whose citizens must now travel to the United States to buy jeans, which are ridiculously overpriced in their homeland. The word **jeans** was derived from the French pronunciation of the city of Genoa in Italy, where the cotton fabric was manufactured. **Denim** similarly derives from the name of a city, the French city of Nîmes, where the sturdy, twilled cotton material was once called **serge de Nîmes.**

What periphrases, what labyrinthine circumlocutions would we have been forced into if Australian had not given us the word **kangaroo** to describe those herbivorous marsupials with their powerful legs for leaping and their thick tails for support? Or the word **boomerang,** which we now use as both a noun and a verb?

Wouldn't Sigmund Freud and his first English translators have been at a disadvantage if the Amerindian languages had not supplied them with the word **totem,** or the Polynesian languages with **taboo**?

Somehow it seems appropriate that the Netherlands, the birthplace of Rembrandt, Vermeer, and Van Gogh, should have bequeathed the word **easel** (which is related to the German word **Esel,** meaning "ass," since an easel is, in many ways, a beast of burden, carrying, as it does, the canvas of many an artist). It is to Dutch, too, that we are indebted for the words **etch, sketch,** and **landscape.**

German has given us a vegetative enclosure in which to raise our five-year-olds (**kindergarten**), a long tube through which a person may breathe while swimming facedown in the water (**snorkel**), and a person who cheats people out of money or other assets (**swindler**), as well as the minerals **quartz** and **feldspar,** and the rock **gneiss.**

Two German cities, Hamburg and Frankfurt, have been a boon to fast-food restaurants everywhere, adding the words **hamburger** and **frankfurter** to our linguistic diet. And as for the condiments, the French have supplied us with the words **mustard** and **mayonnaise,** while the Chinese have given us **ketchup.** If we are not always sure how to spell this word, it is probably because the seventeenth-century English sailors who brought ketchup back from Singapore themselves didn't know how the foreign word should be spelled. The original ketchup was a pickled fish sauce called **ke-tsiap.** The Malays borrowed the word but changed the base from fish to mushrooms. It was Americans who added the tomatoes, and Heinz's famous tomato ketchup first hit American grocery stores in 1876. But since there has never been an agreement on how the word should be transliterated from Chinese, there are those who spell and pronounce the word **catsup,** while others prefer **ketchup.**

Häagen-Dazs and Baskin-Robbins are indebted to Arabic via Turkish and Persian for the word **sherbet.** And who was the well-informed executive at Bird's Eye who knew that the word **punch** (the kind you drink, as opposed to the kind you throw) comes from the Sanskrit word for "five" when he named the fruit punch Five-Alive?

From the Spanish, we have borrowed **cafeteria, tornado, alligator, patio,** and **mosquito.** Indirectly, via Spanish, we have borrowed from the Mexicans, West Indians, and Central Americans many native words such as **tomato, potato, hurricane, avocado, barbecue,** and **chocolate.**

The Malay language has given us **bamboo,** not to mention two words seldom heard outside the Bronx or San Diego zoos—**orangutan** and **cassowary.**

The richness of the English language was similarly enhanced when a veritable menagerie of American Indian words, mostly from Algonquian dialects, were officially accepted into our language—**skunk** in 1588, **raccoon** in 1608, **opossum** in 1610, **moose** in 1613, **woodchuck** in 1674, and **chipmunk** in 1832.

English has frequently borrowed familiar words from languages whose names are anything but familiar to speakers of English. **Curry, catamaran, pariah,** and **teak,** for example, come from Tamil and Malayalam, members of the Dravidian family of languages, spoken principally in southern India, Sri Lanka, and Pakistan. **Commando, trek,** and **spoor** are borrowed from Afrikaans, a language closely related to Dutch that is spoken by over four million people in the Republic of South Africa. The names of at least two games, moreover, have been derived from languages whose origins are obscure. **Polo** comes from Balti, a Tibeto-Burmese language of the people of northern Kashmir, and **jai alai** means "merry festival" in Basque, a language spoken by more than half a million people on both sides of the French-Spanish border.

English has pinched from Polish, purloined from Persian, and pilfered from Portuguese.

No modern language, however, has had a longer or more generous history of lending words to English than has French. Beginning shortly after the victory of William the Conqueror at Hastings in 1066, English borrowed from Middle French such words as **beef, rice,** and **corset** in the thirteenth century; **galoshes, dandelion, biscuit,** and **mitten** in the fourteenth century; **salad, porcupine,** and **nuisance** in the fifteenth century; and **mustache, carrot,** and **cashier** in the sixteenth century.

Modern French contributed **avenue, bigot, intrigue,** and **valise** in the seventeenth century. The eighteenth century witnessed the debut in English of such words as **dentist, avalanche, negligee, chowder,** and, appropriately enough, **debut.** In the nineteenth century, **restaurant, chef,** and **canapé** were added to English's linguistic menu, as was the word **menu** itself. And the twentieth century has seen the arrival of **camouflage, discotheque, triage,** and even **franglais,** a word signifying spoken or written French corrupted by the indiscriminate introduction of English words, especially those of American origin. **Franglais** was coined by linguistic purists in France to decry what they considered an alarming recent trend in that country to adopt foreign words. Not surprisingly, the English language, rather than eschewing, wasted no time embracing yet another French word.

In addition to loan-words borrowed from modern languages, there are more than two hundred thousand words in the English language that have been formed from Latin and Greek roots (too many to treat in this book), words whose histories and etymologies are no less tantalizing than the word **tantalize** itself, which is derived from the name of a mythological Greek king who was punished for a sin against the gods by having to stand, forever thirsty and hungry, in water up to his chin, with fruit-laden boughs hanging over his head. Whenever Tantalus bent to drink, the water disappeared; whenever he reached for the fruit, the wind blew the branches just out of reach, leaving him tantalized, unsatisfied for all eternity.

By now it should be clear that our language has always been receptive to foreign linguistic influence, but this in no way indicates that English is decadent, impoverished, or impure, its speakers weak or pathetically unsure of their identity.

Indeed, what makes the English language colorful, what makes it strong, what makes it quite possibly the richest of the world's languages is precisely its diversity, its willingness to borrow, to expand, to accept, to integrate, to admit humbly that it is sometimes inadequate to express thoughts that other languages phrase with ease and felicity.

African Languages

banana (1597), a tropical plant cultivated for its nutritious fingerlike, yellow-skinned fruit, comes via Spanish or Portuguese from a West African language. Both the Wolof and the Malinke languages have the word **banana,** and Vai, a language of Liberia, has the word **bana.** Originally, the word **banana** was restricted to the luscious pulpy fruit, while the word **banano** was used to signify the tree on which the fruit grew. The expression **banana republic** signifies, often disparagingly, a small tropical country, especially in the Western Hemisphere, whose economy depends primarily on tourism and fruit exports. Since the 1960s, the slang word **bananas** has become synonymous with "crazy" or "wildly enthusiastic." In the 1930s, **bananas** was used by mobsters and other underworld figures to indicate that someone was sexually deviant.

banjo (1739), a musical instrument similar to a guitar, having a circular body covered, like a drum, with tightly stretched parchment, and four or five strings, which may be plucked or strummed, is of African origin. It is probably related to the Kimbundu word **mbanza,** a plucked stringed instrument, and to the Brazilian Portuguese **banza.**

chimpanzee (1738) is an anthropoid ape of equatorial Africa that is smaller and more arboreal than a gorilla. It has a brown-to-black coat, a relatively hairless face that bears a close resemblance to that of humans, prominent ears, and hands adapted for knuckle-walking. The word no doubt derives from a Bantu language of the Atlantic coast.

goober (1833), a word used in the southern (and midland) United States to signify a "peanut," is of African origin. It is similar to the Kimbundu **nguba,** which means "peanut."

gumbo (1805), a stew or soup thickened with okra pods and usually made with chicken, seafood, greens, and other vegetables, comes from a Bantu language. It is related to the Umbundu word **ochinggombo** and Luba word **chinggombo,** both of which mean "okra." **Gumbo** also signifies a silty soil, especially in the central United States, that becomes sticky, waxy or soapy, and nonporous when wet.

impala (1875), a large brownish South African antelope, the male of which has slender horns shaped like a lyre, comes from the Zulu word **im-pala** or from a cognate word in another Nguni dialect (Sechwana **p'hala**). The Scottish missionary and explorer David Livingstone (1813–1873) called the animal a **pallah** in his *Travels and Researches in South Africa* (1857).

mumbo jumbo (1738) is a word signifying meaningless incantations or rituals, obscure or nonsensical talk, gibberish. Sometimes, it is used of pretentious language devised to befuddle the listener or obfuscate an issue; sometimes, it indicates an object of superstitious reverence and fear. Perhaps a reduplication of the Kongo word **nzambi,** meaning "god," the word originally referred to a grotesque idol believed to have been worshiped by certain tribes. Mumbo Jumbo is the name of a tutelary god of the western Sudan who fights evil and punishes women especially for breaking tribal laws.

Okra (1679), the name given to a shrub of the mallow family bearing pods that are used in soups and stews, especially in gumbo, with which it is often synonymous, is said to be of West African origin, although its exact source is still unknown. It is related to Twi **nkuruma** and to Igbo **okuru.** Indigenous to Africa, okra is now cultivated in the southern United States.

Voodoo (1868) is the name given to the body of superstitious beliefs and practices of a polytheistic religion deriving from African ancestor worship (but also containing generous helpings of Roman Catholicism). Voodoo, characterized by serpent worship and sacrificial rites, is practiced largely in the West Indies, especially Haiti, and in the southern United States. The word **voodoo** first appears as **vandoo** and **vandoux** in Louisiana French, but ultimately derives from a West African source, perhaps akin to Ewe **vodu,** "tutelary god, demon."

Zombie (1819), in voodoo, is a soulless corpse—the body of a dead person who, speechless and will-less, has been reanimated by a supernatural force, usually for some evil purpose. The word also refers, informally, to any person whose behavior seems as apathetic, slow-witted, unresponsive, and wooden as that of a zombie. It is the name, too, of a mixed drink made with several kinds of rum, fruit juice, and often apricot liqueur. During World War II, in Canada, the word **zombie** was used, in military slang, as a contemptuous term for one drafted into the army and assigned to home duty. The word **zombie** is of West African origin, from Kongo or Kimbundu **nzambi,** "god," and often refers to a voodoo snake deity. Zombies have become popular in Hollywood movies, where they tend to shamble along with glazed eyes, looking horrible but invariably too slow to cause any real damage. Some of the classics of the zombie genre: Victor Halperin's eerie *White Zombie* (1932), starring Bela Lugosi, about an army of zombies at a sugar mill working for a white leader; Victor Halperin's *Revolt of the Zombies* (1936), in which Dean Jagger reanimates dead Cambodian soldiers to do his bidding; *The Zombies of Mora Tau* (1957), about zombies who guard diamonds hidden in a sunken ship; and Jacques Tourneur's masterful *I Walked with a Zombie* (1943), set on a Caribbean island and based loosely on *Jane Eyre*. In the late 1960s, George A. Romero revived the genre with such delightfully repellent cinematic gems as *Night of the Living Dead* (1968), frequently called "the best film ever made in Pittsburgh," in which seven people barricade themselves inside a farmhouse to escape legions of carnivorous zombies reanimated by radiation, and *Dawn of the Dead* (1979), a savage satire on consumerism, about several people trapped inside a shopping center by a horde of flesh-eating zombies.

Afrikaans

aardvark (1833), a nocturnal, burrowing mammal about the size of a badger found in central and southern Africa, comes from Afrikaans **erdvark,** which is related to Dutch **aardvarken,** meaning "earth pig." The aardvark, occupying a position between the armadillo and the anteater, feeds on ants and termites, and has a long extensile tongue, powerful claws, and long ears.

commando (1791), the name applied to any member of a military assault team trained to move with lightning speed in urgent, threatening situations, as, for example, against terrorists holding hostages, comes from Afrikaans **kommando,** meaning "raid, raiding party," itself from Portuguese **commando** from the verb **commandar,** "to command." During World War II, commandos were shock troops—Allied military units specially trained and organized for hit-and-run raids into Axis territories. Earlier still, the word was used in South Africa to signify quasi-military expeditions of the Portuguese and especially of the Dutch Boers against the natives.

spoor (1823), the track or trail of a person or animal, especially that of a wild animal pursued as game, comes from Afrikaans. In the nineteenth century, the word was sometimes used in English to mean "the track of a vehicle."

trek (1821), to travel or migrate, usually in an organized way but slowly or with difficulty, or (in South Africa) to make a journey by ox wagon, comes from Afrikaans and is related to the Dutch word **trek,** "a draw, pull, tug, march," from the verb **trekken,** "to draw [a vehicle], to tug, to tow, to pull, to travel."

Arabic

admiral (1205) was first used in English with the now obsolete meaning of "an emir or prince under the Sultan" and indicated any Saracen or "infidel" ruler or commander. By the fifteenth century, the word referred to the commander-in-chief of the fleet of a country or to a naval officer of the highest rank. It comes from the Arabic **amir al,** meaning "commander of," and occurs in many titles in Arabic, as, for example, **amir-al-umara,** "commander of rulers"; **amir-al-mā,** "commander of the water"; and **amir-al-bahr,** "commander of the sea." The letter **d** was added because of a confusion with the Latin word **admirabilis,** "able to be viewed with wonder."

albacore (1579), a large sea tuna with long pectoral fins, the flesh of which is valued for canning, comes via Portuguese from Arabic **al-bakūrah,** "the tuna."

albatross (1564), the name given to various large web-footed seabirds, comes from the Arabic **al qadus,** which denotes "a bucket affixed to a water wheel used for irrigation." The word came into English through Spanish, where the Arabic word had entered as **arcaduz,** signifying "a bucket or conduit," and as **alcatraz,** meaning "pelican." The pelican, with its huge bucketlike bill, was believed to collect water in its beak to carry to its young in the desert. Perhaps the most famous of all albatrosses is the bird that hung "instead of a cross" about the neck of Samuel Taylor Coleridge's Ancient Mariner. Alcatraz, the island in San Francisco Bay famous for its virtually escapeproof federal prison, was so named by early Spanish settlers in the Americas because of its large pelican population.

alchemy (1362), a medieval form of chemistry and speculative philosophy that was concerned primarily with discovering ways of transmuting base metals into gold, of finding a universal cure for disease and an elixir to prolong life indefinitely, comes from Arabic **al**, "the," and **kimiya**, which is derived, in turn, from late Greek **kemeia**, "transmutation."

alcohol (1672) is a colorless, volatile, flammable liquid with an etherlike odor and a pungent, burning taste. The intoxicating agent in fermented and distilled liquors, such as whiskey, gin, and vodka, it is also used in medicines, lotions, colognes, rocket fuel, and automobile radiation antifreeze. Originally, it was the fine metallic powder used in the East to stain the eyelids and, by extension, any fine powder, such as alcohol of brimstone and the alcohol of the spleen of an ass. It comes from Arabic **al-kuh'l,** which means "powdered antimony" or "collyrium."

alcove (1676), a recess or small room next to or opening out of a room, a nook, comes, via Spanish, from Arabic **al-gobbah,** "the dome vault." The word is also used in English to signify a covered retreat, a bower or summerhouse in a garden, or an arched recess or niche in a wall for a bed or bookcases.

alfalfa (1845), a plant of the legume family originating in the Near East and widely grown for hay and forage, comes, via Spanish, from Arabic **al-fasfasah.** Charles Darwin was the first writer to use the word in English.

algebra (1551) comes from the Arabic **al-jebr,** "the reunion or reintegration of broken parts," and originally referred to the surgical treatment of bone fractures. It also referred to the science of "integration and equation," which was the Arabic term for algebraic computation. There is a fanciful but specious tradition that derives the word from the name of a famous Arab chemist named Geber, mentioned by Richard Burton in his *Anatomy of Melancholy* (1621). The word **algebra** was still being used in English in the sixteenth and early seventeenth centuries to refer to the art of bone setting. Today, however, the word refers only to the branch of mathematics that investigates the relations and properties of numbers by means of symbols.

almanac (c. 1391), a publication containing data for the coming year, such as the times of sunrises and sunsets, phases of the moon, tides, and other statistical information, comes from Arabic **al-manākh,** "the calendar." The word appears in Latin (in Roger Bacon's *Opus Majus*) and in Italian (Giovanni Villani's *Cronica*) before it is recorded in English (in Chaucer). Today, the word also refers to an annual reference book full of interesting facts relating to countries of the world, natural disasters, sports, entertainment, and so forth. The very first American almanac, *An Almanak for the Year of Our Lord 1639, Calculated for New England,* was written by William Pierce and published in Cambridge, Massachusetts.

apricot (1551), a fuzzy, yellowish pink fruit resembling a peach and plum in flavor, comes, via French and Spanish, from Arabic **al-barqūq,** which came, via Greek, from a Latin word meaning "early-ripening [peach]."

arsenal (1506), a place where arms and military equipment for land or naval service are manufactured or stored, comes from Arabic **dar asina'ah,** "house of mechanical industry, workshop, factory." The word is now used more loosely to indicate any collection of weapons, dockyard, or repertory.

artichoke (1531) is the name of a tall, thistlelike plant found in the Mediterranean area. Its immature flower head and the fleshy bases of its leaves are eaten as a vegetable. Although it is borrowed from Arabic **al-kharshuf** via Upper Italian **articiocco,** there is an early English tradition, plausible but erroneous, that says that the artichoke gets its name from the fact that it **chokes** the garden or the heart.

assassin (1603), a person who attempts to murder another, usually an important public figure, by stealthy violence, comes from the Arabic **hashshashin,** literally "hashish-eaters, those addicted to [smoking or chewing] hashish." It originally referred to the Ismaili fanatics of the Shiite branch of Muslims, who used to intoxicate themselves with a powder made of hemp (or hashish) before their murderous attacks on the Seljuks, the Turkish rulers of Persia, Syria, and Asia Minor before the Ottomans, or on the Christians in the time of the Crusades.

caliber (1567), the diameter of any body of circular section, especially that of the inside of a tube or hollow cylinder, such as the bore of a gun, is borrowed from Arabic **qālib,** "mold, shoemaker's last." The word also signifies the degree of one's merit, excellence, importance, rank, or social standing.

candy (c. 1420), any confection made with syrup or crystallized sugar, made by repeated boiling and evaporation, and combined with fruit, nuts, chocolate, and the like, comes into English from Arabic **qandi,** "sugar," which may be related to Sanskrit **khandakah,** "sugar in crystalline pieces," from **khanda,** "piece," from the verb **khand,** "to break."

carafe (1786), a wide-mouthed glass bottle with a flaring lip used for holding liquids and serving beverages, comes, via French and Italian, from Arabic **gharrāfah,** "dipper, drinking vessel," which is related to several other Arabic words, like **gharafa,** "to draw or lift water"; **ghuruf,** "little cup"; and **gharrāf,** "having much water."

caraway (c. 1300), an annual or biennial plant of the carrot family with white flowers and small aromatic fruits called "caraway seeds," is borrowed from the Arabic **karawiya.** Caraway seeds are used in cakes, breads, beverages, and medicines, and also in pickling.

Cipher (1399) comes from the Arabic **sifr,** "nought, zero," a noun use of an adjective meaning "empty" or "void," which, in turn, is a translation of the Sanskrit word **sūnyā,** "empty." The word has several meanings in English: zero, a secret code, a nonentity or person of no influence, and something of no value.

Coffee (1598) comes, via Italian and Turkish, from Arabic **qah-wah,** the name of the beverage made by percolation, infusion, or decoction from the roasted, ground, or crushed seeds of the two-seeded fruit of certain trees or shrubs of the madder family. Arabic lexicographers assert that the word originally meant "wine" and is derived from **qahiya,** "to have no appetite."

Cotton (c. 1300), a soft, white fibrous substance consisting of the fibers surrounding the seeds of plants of the mallow family that is used in making cloth and thread, comes from Arabic **qutun.**

Crimson (c. 1400), meaning deep purplish red, comes from Arabic **qirmizi.** The English word **carmine,** which signifies both a purplish red color and a beautiful red pigment obtained from the dried bodies of female cochineal insects, comes from the same Arabic word. The English word **kermes,** which, like **carmine,** refers to a red dye prepared from dried female insect bodies (living on evergreen oaks of the Mediterranean region), is likewise derived from **qirmizi.**

elixir (c. 1386) is a word originally applied to two alchemical drugs or essences believed to be capable of prolonging life indefinitely or of changing base metals into gold. Today, **elixir** signifies a sweetened liquid containing alcohol that is used as a vehicle for medicinal agents. The word is borrowed from Arabic **al-iksir,** "the preparation," which comes ultimately from the Greek word **xerion,** a drying powder for wounds. The Xerox Corporation derives its name, incidentally, from the Greek word **xeros,** "dry."

g **houl** (1786) is an evil spirit believed to feed on human flesh, robbing graves and preying on corpses. From Arabic **ghūl,** "one who seizes," the word is now also applied to human grave robbers or to people who take an unusual delight in things that are revolting. Edgar Allan Poe wrote of "the ghoul-haunted woodland of Weir" in his 1849 poem "Ulalume."

h **azard** (c. 1300), from Arabic **al-zahr,** "the die," can signify an unavoidable danger or risk, a chance event, an accident, uncertainty, the lack of predictability, or a game played with two dice in which the chances are complicated by an involved set of rules, the forerunner of craps. In Shakespeare's *Henry V,* when the French lord Rambures asks, "Who will go to Hazard with me for twenty prisoners?" he is clearly referring to the game of chance. In the same play, **hazard** is used as a tennis term, referring to an opening in the walls of an old-fashioned tennis court that rendered any ball that entered it "dead." Today, it also refers to a golf-course obstacle.

j **ar** (1592), an often cylindrical vessel of earthenware, stoneware, or glass, without a spout or handle (or with two handles), is borrowed from Arabic **jarrah,** "earthen water vessel."

k **ismet** (1849), fate or destiny, comes, via Turkish and Persian, from Arabic **qismah,** "division, portion, lot, fate," and is related to the Arabic verb **qasama,** "to divide." *Kismet* is the name of a 1953 Broadway musical starring Alfred Drake and Doretta Morrow, with music adapted from themes composed by the Russian composer Alexander Borodin.

l **ilac** (1625), a shrub of the olive family cultivated for its fragrant pale pinkish violet or white blossoms, comes from Arabic **lilak,** which is a variation of Persian **nīlak,** "bluish" (from **nīl,** "blue"), and Sanskrit **nīla,** "dark blue."

lime (1638), a small greenish citrus fruit related to the lemon, comes, via French or Spanish, from Arabic līmah, "citrus fruit." The slang expression **limey,** applied to British sailors or to Englishmen in general, originated in a British Navy custom, begun in the late eighteenth century, of distributing a daily ration of lime juice to all sailors on active duty in order to prevent scurvy. Australian and American sailors subsequently called the British "lime-juicers," which was eventually shortened to "limeys." There is no etymological connection between **lime,** the citrus fruit, and **lime,** the grayish white water-soluble solid used to make plasters and cements.

macramé (1869), a coarse, elaborate lacelike webbing or fringe made by knotting cords or yarn in geometrical patterns, comes, via French or Italian and Turkish, from Arabic **miqramah,** "embroidered coverlet or veil."

magazine (1583) comes, via French and Italian, from Arabic **makhāzin,** the plural of **makhzan,** "storehouse," which is related to the verb **khazana,** "to store up." The word signifies a repository or warehouse where goods are stored; the chamber of a repeating rifle or machine gun; a building for keeping military supplies; and, beginning in the eighteenth century, a periodical publication containing essays, stories, and poems by various writers. The word **magazine** was first used in periodical titles in 1731, when *The Gentleman's Magazine: or, Monthly Intelligencer* was published as a "storehouse of information."

marzipan (1494), also called **marchpane,** a confection made of crushed almonds or almond paste, sugar, and egg whites, and usually molded into various shapes, as, for example, coins and tiny fruits and vegetables, comes, via German **Marzipan** and Italian **marzapane,** "small box, medieval coin," from Arabic **mawthabān,** "medieval coin, seated king." It has been suggested that the "coin" sense of the word may be the source of all the other meanings. There was a medieval Venetian coin, a **matapanus,** which bore the figure of Jesus Christ on a throne. Saracens, in contact with the Venetians, no doubt used the Arabic word **maw-thabān** as a derisive name for this coin.

monsoon (1584), from Arabic **mawsim,** "season," related to the verb **wasama,** "to mark," is the name given to a seasonal wind, commonly accompanied by heavy and continuous rainfall, that blows over southern Asia and especially in the Indian Ocean from the southwest in summer and from the northeast in winter. The monsoon ushers in the rainy season in India.

mufti (1586), from Arabic **mufti,** "one who delivers a judgment," the present active participle of **aftā,** "to give a decision [on a point of law]," was first used in English in the sixteenth century to signify a Muslim priest or expounder of the law. By 1816, the word had also come to signify civilian clothes in contrast to military clothes, or plain clothes worn by anyone who has a right to wear a uniform, as in the expression "in mufti."

nadir (c. 1391) is used both of a point in the heavens diametrically opposed to some other point, especially the sun, and of the point of the heavens diametrically opposite to the zenith. Thus, it has also come to mean the lowest point, the point of greatest adversity. It is borrowed from Arabic **nadir,** "over against, opposite to [the zenith]."

racket (1500), from Arabic **rāhet,** a variation of **rāhah,** "palm of the hand," is a short-handled paddle used to hit a Ping-Pong ball, or a lightweight implement with a netting of catgut or nylon stretched across a somewhat elliptical frame used for striking the ball or shuttlecock in such games as tennis, squash, and badminton. The word has also been applied to certain snowshoes used in North America.

ream (1481) is borrowed, via Spanish, from Arabic **rizmah,** "bale, bundle (of clothes, paper, and so forth)." The word is applied to a standard quantity of paper, consisting of 20 quires (480 sheets) or sometimes 500 sheets (to allow for waste). In the plural, it also means a large quantity, usually of paper, without reference to the precise number of sheets.

sash (1590), from Arabic **shāsh,** is a scarf or band worn by men over one shoulder or around the waist, usually as part of a military uniform, or by women and children around the waist, simply for decoration.

sherbet (1603) is a frozen fruit mixture, similar to an ice, but usually with milk, egg whites, or gelatin added. It originally signified (and still does in Great Britain and the Near East) a cooling drink made of sweetened fruit juice, as its etymology suggests: it is borrowed, via Turkish and Persian, from Arabic **sharbah,** "a drink." In 1615, costly sherbets sold in Constantinople were made not only from sugar and lemons, but also from violets.

sofa (1625) is a long upholstered couch, with a back and ends, used for reclining. In Eastern countries, it is a part of the floor raised, sometimes as high as two feet, and covered with rich carpets. The word **sofa** first entered the English language in the latter sense, as its derivation, from Arabic **suffah,** "platform used as a seat," would imply.

spinach (1530), a green plant cultivated for its succulent, edible leaves, is believed to come from Arabic **isfānākh.**

S umac (c. 1400), a shrub or small tree belonging to the cashew family with milky sap and small, fleshy fruit, comes from Arabic **summāq**. The dried and powdered leaves and shoots of the plant are used in tanning, for staining leather black, and medicinally as an astringent.

S yrup (1398), from Arabic **sharāb**, "a drink," originally used of wine and other beverages in Arab countries, now signifies a thick, sweet liquid, prepared from molasses, glucose, and water, and sometimes fruit juices, and used in cookery—for example, as a topping for pancakes and ice-cream sundaes. It is also used as a vehicle for medicines.

t alc (1601), from Arabic **talq**, "mica," was originally applied by Arabs to any of various transparent, translucent, or shining minerals, such as mica, talc proper, and selenite. The word is first found in English in a translation of the Roman writer Pliny's *Natural History*, in a section on beehives made of talc, "which is a kind of transparent glasse stone, because they would see through them how the Bees do worke and labor within." Today, it refers to magnesium silicate, the whitish, greenish, or grayish soft mineral, with a soapy feel, that is used to make lubricants, talcum powder, and electrical insulation.

t ariff (1592), an official list or schedule enumerating the duties or customs imposed by a government on imports or exports, comes, via Italian **tariffa**, from Arabic **ta'rīfah**, "notification, explanation."

Z enith (1387), the highest point of the sky directly overhead, the culmination or acme, the apex or summit, comes from Old Spanish **zenit**, a modification of Arabic **samt**, "way, path, road," which is short for **samt ar-rās**, "the way or road above one's head."

Zero (1604), which, like the English word **cipher,** is derived from the Arabic **sifr,** "cipher," is the figure 0, which in the Arabic notation for numbers stands for the absence of quantity, for naught, for nothing.

Australian

boomerang (1827), a bent or curved piece of hardwood (with a sharp edge along the convexity of the curve) used by the Australian Aborigines as a throwing club, one designed in such a way that it returns to the thrower, comes from Dharuk **bumarin.** The word now also signifies an argument or scheme that backfires on its originator. When Captain Cook first laid eyes on a boomerang at Botany Bay, he thought it resembled a Turkish scimitar and concluded that it was a wooden sword.

kangaroo (1770), a herbivorous marsupial mammal of Australia, Tasmania, and Papua with a small head, short forelimbs, a long tail, and powerful hindquarters used for leaping, comes from **gang-urru,** the name given to the large black or gray species of kangaroo in Guugu Yimidhiir, an Australian Aboriginal language spoken around Cookstown in North Queensland. The first species known in Europe was the great kangaroo, the male of which stands about six feet tall.

Wombat (1798), from Dharuk **wom-bat,** is a burrowing, herbivorous marsupial with a thick, heavy body and short legs. It is about the size of a badger and resembles a small bear.

Basque

Chaparral (1850), the term used in the southwestern United States for a dense tangled growth of shrubs or small evergreen trees, is derived, via Spanish **chaparro,** "evergreen oak" (from Basque **tshapar**), and **-al,** a Spanish collective suffix for a grove or collection of trees.

jai alai (1903) is perhaps the only word in English to come directly from Basque, the language of the people of obscure origin who live in the western Pyrenees on the Bay of Biscay. **Jai alai,** deriving from **jai,** "festival," and **alai,** "merry," is a court game resembling handball played by two or four players with a small ball and a long, curved wicker basket strapped to one arm. Many historians believe that the game was invented in Spain in 1518 by Ignatius of Loyola, the Basque soldier-saint who founded the Jesuit order.

Celtic Languages

banshee (1771), a spirit in Irish folklore who assumes the form of a woman who wails under the windows of a house as a sign that one of the members of the household is about to die, comes from Irish **bean sidhe,** "woman of the fairy folk." The banshee appears either as a beautiful woman who weeps for the coming death or as a hideous hag who prophesies it. She is similar to the Washer of the Ford, a woman who is seen washing bloody clothes in a river by someone who is doomed to die shortly.

bard (c. 1450), from Irish/Scotch Gaelic **bard,** "poet-singer, minstrel," was originally used of poets who composed and recited epic or heroic tales of chiefs and warriors. Now, the word generally signifies any poet. In Wales today, **bard** has a more specific meaning: it is applied to a poet or versifier who has been recognized at the Eisteddfod "session," an annual festival consisting of competitions among musicians and poets.

b**rogue** (1586), from Irish Gaelic **brog,** "shoe," a word derived ultimately from Latin **bracae,** "trousers," started out in English as a coarse shoe made of untanned leather worn by the inhabitants of the wilder parts of Scotland and Ireland. By 1705, the word was being applied to an Irish accent in the pronunciation of English, presumably because those who wore brogues or called their shoes "brogues" tended to speak with a noticeable Irish accent.

c**lan** (c. 1425), a group of families or households whose heads claim descent from a common ancestor, comes from Scotch Gaelic **clann,** "offspring," which is borrowed from Latin **planta,** "sprout, shoot, scion." Anthropologists today consider clans to be the principal social units of tribal organization. The word **clan** is also often synonymous with **clique** or **party** and is used especially of a group of people united by some common trait.

f**lummery** (1623), from Welsh **llymru,** is the name of various dishes made of flour, milk, eggs, and sugar. It can be oatmeal boiled with water until thick or a fruit custard (or blancmange) thickened with cornstarch. Since 1749, the word has also come to signify total nonsense, empty compliments and mere flattery, or complete humbug.

g**alore** (1675), an adverb in English meaning "in abundance" or "in plentiful amounts," comes from Irish Gaelic **go leor,** "enough or plenty."

penguin (1578), from Welsh **pen gwyn,** "white head," is a flightless, waddling aquatic bird with webbed feet and wings reduced to scaly flippers or paddles with which it swims underwater. Penguins inhabit the Southern Hemisphere, living on Antarctica and on islands off South Africa, South America, Australia, and New Zealand. The name "white head" originally referred to the great auk in its white winter plumage and was misapplied to penguins. By 1578, the word was already applied to the birds we call penguins, which were found by Sir Francis Drake at the Strait of Magellan.

phony (1900), as an adjective, means "not real, fake, and counterfeit," "insincere and pretentious," and "false and deceiving." As a noun, it means "someone who is insincere, pretentious, or deceitful, or something that is false or counterfeit." The word perhaps comes from Irish Gaelic **fawney,** "finger ring," and refers to a confidence game in which a brass ring is sold as a gold one.

plaid (1512), from Scotch Gaelic **plaide** (related to Irish Gaelic **ploid**), "blanket," is a fabric woven of different-colored yarns in a crossbarred pattern. The word also refers, more specifically, to a long rectangular piece of woolen cloth with a checkered or tartan pattern worn across the left shoulder by Scottish Highlanders, originally in cold or stormy weather.

Shebang (1867), as in the expression "the whole shebang," signifies any matter of present concern, the structure of an organization, of a contrivance, or affair. Although the word's origin is obscure, one suggestion is that it comes from Irish Gaelic **shebeen,** a tavern where illicit whiskey is sold.

Slogan (1513), from Scotch Gaelic **sluagh-ghairm,** "army cry or shout," is either the distinctive note, phrase, or motto—the catchword—of an organization, manufacturer, or person or, less frequently, a battle cry, as that formerly raised by the Scottish Highlanders.

Whiskey (1715), an alcoholic liquor distilled from the fermented mash of grains, such as rye, barley, or corn, is derived from Irish Gaelic **uisce beatha** or Scotch Gaelic **uisge beatha,** which is, ultimately, a translation of Latin **aqua vitae,** "water of life." The word **usquebaugh** is still used of Irish and Scotch whiskey.

Chinese

gung-ho (1942), an English adjective meaning "wholeheartedly enthusiastic, eager, zealous, and loyal," was introduced into English as a training slogan by a United States Marine officer, Evans F. Carlson (1896–1947), during the Second World War. It is borrowed from Chinese **kung ho,** "work together," which is short for **chung-kuo-kung-yeh-ho-tso she,** the name of the Chinese Industrial Cooperative Society.

ketchup (1711), also spelled **catsup,** comes from Malay **ke-chap,** "fish sauce," which may come, in turn, from Chinese (Amoy dialect) **ke-tsiap,** "brine of pickled fish or shellfish." The spelling varies because the English sailors and merchants who brought the sauce back from Singapore could not agree on how the word sounded, and hence on how it should be transliterated. Although most Americans think of ketchup as a condiment consisting of pureed tomatoes, with onions, vinegar, sugar, salt, and various spices, the word may be used of various other condiments, as, for example, walnut ketchup and mushroom ketchup. It was, in fact,

Americans who first added the tomatoes. In 1876, tomato ketchup became the first important product of the H. J. Heinz Company, established seven years earlier.

kowtow (1804), to act in an obsequiously respectful way or to show excessive deference, comes from Chinese **kou tou,** "knock (one's) head." It is derived from the Chinese custom of touching the ground with one's forehead while kneeling or prostrating oneself as an act of extreme respect, submission, apology, or worship.

mah-jongg (1922) is an old Chinese game introduced into Europe and America in the early 1920s. The 144 (or sometimes 136) dominolike pieces used in the game are called tiles, and they are divided into five or six suits. The players, usually numbering four, have to build a hand containing four sets of three tiles and a pair. The word comes from Guangdong (Cantonese) dialect **mah-jeuk,** "sparrow" or "hemp bird," and is so named from the sparrow depicted on the first tile of a set. The game became a great fad among women in the United States from 1922 to 1925, outselling radios, causing a shortage of calf shinbones in China (used to make the tiles), and inspiring an Eddie Cantor song, "Since Ma Is Playing Mah-Jongg." By 1926, the fad ended (supplanted by crossword puzzles, the new national craze), and not a few game importers went bankrupt.

pekoe (1712), a highly popular kind of black tea made from leaves coarser than those used for orange pekoe, is derived from Amoy (Chinese) dialect **pek-ho,** meaning either "white empress" or "white hair, white down," the latter suggesting that the tea derived its name from the leaves' being picked young with the down still on them.

t ea (c. 1655), the dried and prepared leaves of a fragrant white-flowered shrub from which an aromatic beverage is prepared by infusion in hot water, is borrowed either from the Xiamen dialect **t'e** or from the Amoy dialect **te.** The Portuguese, trading in Macao, introduced the form **cha,** which is Cantonese as well as Mandarin Chinese, into several European languages. It was, however, the Dutch, who bought their tea in Bantam and Formosa (where the Amoy word was used), that brought the form **te** into Dutch (and French) and eventually into English.

t yphoon (1588), the name given to a tropical cyclone, tempest, or hurricane in the region of the Philippines or the China seas, occurring chiefly from July to October, or, sometimes, to a violent storm of India, comes from Chinese dialect **tai fung,** "big wind" (equivalent to Chinese **da,** "big," and **feng,** "wind"), altered because of its similarity to the Greek **typhon,** "violent wind."

Creole

b ayou (1766) is an arm or offshoot, an inlet, or outlet of a lake, river, or other body of water, that is usually marshy, sluggish, and stagnant. The word, used mostly in the Lower Mississippi Valley region and the Gulf States, comes from Creole **bayou** (probably from Choctaw **bayuk**) and means "river forming part of a delta."

j azz (1909) is the term applied to American music that originated in New Orleans at the beginning of the twentieth century. Rooted in ragtime and blues, jazz is characterized by syncopated rhythms, polyphonic ensemble playing, improvisation, virtuoso solos, melodic freedom, and deliberate distortions of pitch and timbre. **Jazz** is sometimes said to come from a vulgar Creole word meaning "to copulate," commonly used in New Orleans dance halls in the

1890s. Some claim that it comes from black patois (of African origin) meaning "to excite," with an erotic and rhythmic connotation; others, that it comes from a Creole word meaning "to speed up." Perhaps the most intriguing etymology has jazz deriving its name from Jasbo Brown, an itinerant black musician who performed along the Mississippi and, later, in Chicago cabarets.

Czech

robot (1923) derives from the Czech word **robota** ("work, toil"). The word was first popularized by the play *R.U.R.* (which stood for "Rossum's Universal Robots"), a symbolic fantasy written by Karel Capek in 1921. In the play, a robot factory produces mechanical androids intended to free human beings from manual labor and serve as their slaves. Endowed with human feelings by Dr. Gall, a cynical and irresponsible scientist, the robots revolt, overthrow their human masters, and wipe out all but one of them, a mason named Alquist. In so doing, however, they doom themselves to extinction, since the formula for creating new robots is destroyed. The play ends optimistically when two of the robots, Primus and Helena, show that they understand the concepts of love and self-sacrifice and venture forth as the Adam and Eve of the new robot age.

Dravidian Languages

catamaran (1697), a sailing raft formed of two or more logs or pieces of wood lashed together, usually propelled by a sail, and used for short distances, comes from Tamil **kattamaram,** "tied wood."

Curry (1598), from Tamil **kari,** "sauce, relish (for rice)," is a pungent dish of vegetables, onions, fish, or meat cooked with various ground spices such as cayenne powder, fenugreek, and turmeric and frequently served with rice.

mulligatawny (1784), a highly seasoned, curry-flavored East Indian soup made with chicken or meat stock, is borrowed from Tamil **milakutannir,** "pepper water."

pariah (1613) is borrowed from the Tamil language of India, where the word **parai** refers to a large drum. The pariahs, or **paraiyar** ("drummers"), were members of a Dravidian group who beat the drums at certain festivals. The pariahs, especially numerous in Madras, ignored Hindu precepts regarding purity: they routinely handled forbidden foods and dirty laundry, and were often employed as shoemakers or in other forbidden professions. They were ranked so low in the caste system, in fact, that even the lowest caste of Brahmans had to avoid them. Shortly after the word **pariah** entered the English language, it came to include any person to be shunned or avoided, any social outcast. The English colonials in India were, for the most part, totally unaware of the complexities of the caste system and perceived only that the Brahmans, who were Indo-European (or Aryan), shrank from any contact with the Paraiyar, who were of non–Indo-European origin and therefore considered inferior. Taking advantage of the situation, the English regularly hired and underpaid these "unclean" pariahs as domestics in their households. The word **pariah** was also used derogatorily in combination with other words. For example, there was an unwholesome native liquor made in India that was called **pariah-arrack,** a scavenger bird named the **pariah-kite,** and a yellowish dog of low breed that wandered into towns and villages called the **pariah-dog.**

Dutch and Flemish

boor (1551), an unmannerly person, a country bumpkin, a rude or insensitive individual, is derived from Dutch **boer,** "peasant, farmer, fellow-occupier of a dwelling, especially a farm," related to the verb **bouwen,** "to inhabit, to cultivate, to till," since it was assumed that farmers were rude and ill-bred. **Boor** is related etymologically to the German word for farmer, **Bauer,** and also to the **bor** in the English word **neighbor,** which means "near-dweller." The Boers of South Africa (of Dutch or Huguenot descent) were, as their name suggests, originally farmers.

booze (c. 1300), a term applied for almost seven hundred years to alcoholic beverages, such as whiskey, or to drinking bouts, comes from Middle Dutch **busen** or **buizen,** "to drink to excess."

boss (1650), a person who employs workers, a manager, a politician who controls the party machine, or, sometimes, anyone who has the right to give orders, comes from Dutch **baas,** which means "master or foreman," but originally meant "uncle."

bowery (1650), from Dutch **bouwerij,** "farm, husbandry," is a word that signified a farm or plantation to the Dutch settlers of New York. It now refers specifically to a street and a squalid area of New York City, the Bowery, known for its cheap hotels and places of entertainment and peopled by the homeless. As early as 1840, the *Daily Picayune* of New Orleans was reporting that "the Bowery boys of New York have . . . eclipsed the nice young men of Baltimore." The expression **Bowery boy** describes the rough and rowdy young men raised in the Bowery. In the 1940s and 1950s, the Bowery Boys, a splinter group from the Dead End Kids of Sidney Kingsley's tenement drama *Dead End,* became the main characters in many cheaply made but extremely popular second features at the movies. Brooklyn hoodlums who became lovable slapstick comedians, they searched for uranium and diamonds, and battled everything from mobsters, smugglers, and vampires to a man-eating plant.

brandy (1657) is a spirit distilled from wine or from fermented fruit juices, as of grapes, apples, plums, and peaches. **Brandy** is short for **brandywine,** from Dutch **brandewijn,** "burnt (distilled) wine." Although the fuller form **brandywine** was retained in official use, as in the imposing of duties and tariffs, until the beginning of the eighteenth century, the word was commonly abbreviated to **brandy** by 1657.

bumpkin (1570), an awkward, unsophisticated yokel, comes from Dutch **boomken,** "little tree," or, more probably, from Middle Dutch **bommekijn,** "little barrel or beam." **Bumpkin** was originally a humorous appellation for a Dutchman, especially one whose build was short and stumpy.

caboose (1769), the name of the car on a freight train used by the workmen, often as their quarters, and now invariably located at the rear of the train, is derived from Dutch **kabuis,** "ship's gallery, storeroom." Originally, the word signified, even in English, the cookroom or kitchen on merchant ships or fishing boats.

coleslaw (1794), from Dutch **koolsla,** "cabbage salad," is sliced or chopped raw cabbage dressed with salt, pepper, vinegar, and mayonnaise. The word makes an early appearance in one of the most unlikely places, James Fenimore Cooper's 1822 novel *The Spy:* "Potatoes, onions, beets, cold-slaw, rice and all the other minutiae of a goodly dinner."

cookie (1703), from Dutch **koekie,** "little cake," is a small, flat, sweet cake made from stiff dough rolled and sliced or dropped onto a large flat pan and baked.

cruise (1651) can mean "to sail around on a pleasure trip," "to fly, drive, or sail at a constant speed," or "to travel about slowly looking for customers or sexual partners." It is borrowed from Dutch **kruisen,** "to cross," related to the noun **kruis,** "cross."

decoy (1626), an animal (often a bird) that is trained to lure or entice another animal, often of its own species, into a trap or within gunshot. The word is used, too, of artificial birds, like wooden ducks, used for the same purpose. A decoy can also be a person who lures another person into some trap or dangerous situation. **Decoy** comes from Dutch **de kooi,** "the cage."

dope (1807), any thick liquid or semiliquid used as a lubricant or to coat fabrics or other materials in order to make them waterproof or stronger. By 1851, the word was used of a stupid or unresponsive person. By 1889, it was applied, too, to illicit, habit-forming narcotic drugs, such as opium and heroin. By 1901, the word was synonymous with information or news. **Dope** comes from Dutch **doop,** "sauce," which is related to the verb **doopen,** "to dip."

easel (1634) is a wooden frame for supporting an artist's canvas while the painter is at work on it, or for displaying at an angle a porcelain plate or a blackboard. **Easel** is borrowed from Dutch **ezel,** "ass," a beast of burden employed to carry heavy material in much the same way that an easel shoulders the artist's canvas. The use, in English, of the word **horse** as a frame with legs used for supporting something (planks, staging, or an Olympic gymnast) is similar.

e **tch** (1634), to engrave copper or other metal plates, glass, or stone by corroding the surface with acids or other agents to form a design that, when charged with ink, will leave an impression on paper, comes from Dutch **etsen,** "to cause to eat" or "to cause to be eaten."

f **rolic** (1538), merriment, a prank, playful behavior, comes from Dutch **vrolijk,** "joyful."

f **urlough** (1625), a vacation or leave of absence granted to an enlisted person in the military to be absent from duty for a stated time, is borrowed from Dutch **verlof,** "leave, permission."

g **herkin** (1661), a small, immature variety of cucumber used in pickling, comes from Dutch **gurken,** the plural of **gurk,** "cucumber." The first English writer to use the word was Samuel Pepys, who wrote in his diary for December 1, 1661, "We . . . opened the glass of girkins . . . which are rare things."

h **owitzer** (1695), a cannon having a relatively short barrel, used for the firing of projectiles with small charges and relatively high trajectories to reach targets behind cover, comes from Dutch **houwitser,** which, in turn, comes from Czech **houfnice,** "slingshot, catapult."

h **ustle** (1684), from Dutch **husselen,** "to shake, to toss," means "to proceed or work rapidly," "to be aggressive in business," "to sell or promote energetically," or "to engage in prostitution." In the eighteenth century, it meant "to push or knock a person about roughly," as in Tobias Smollett's 1751 novel *Peregrine Pickle*: "I was hussled by those rebellious rapscallions." The noun **hustler** became popular in the nineteenth century as one who takes part in hustling a person, specifically, a member of a gang of pickpockets. Today, it also signifies a swindler who uses fraudulent methods to obtain money or a gambler who preys on unsuspecting amateur challengers in order to win money from them. One of the best films of the 1960s was Robert Rossen's hard-hitting 1961 drama *The Hustler*, about a talented pool shark (played by Paul Newman) who lacks what it takes to be a winner.

kink (1678), a twist or curl in a rope, thread, wire, or hair, a muscular stiffness in the neck or back, a flaw or imperfection in a machine or plan likely to cause difficulties, is borrowed from Dutch **kink,** "a twist, a twirl."

knapsack (1603), from Dutch **knapzak,** "eating sack," the **knap** derived from the verb **knappen,** "to make a snapping noise, to crack, to bite," is a canvas, nylon, or leather bag for carrying clothes and food that is strapped to the back by hikers and soldiers.

landscape (1598), a picture representing natural inland or rural scenery, as distinguished from a portrait or sea picture, comes from Dutch **landschap,** a word introduced as a technical term of painters. Although the first true landscape paintings can be dated back to the 1340s, when the frescoes in the pope's palace at Avignon were painted, the Netherlands, in the sixteenth and seventeenth centuries, produced some of the world's earliest landscapists, including Pieter Brueghel the Younger, Jacob van Ruisdael, and Rembrandt.

luck (1481), from Middle Dutch **luk,** probably came into English as a gambling term. It is now used to signify good or bad fortune—that is, the force that seems to cause or shape events favorable or unfavorable to the interests of a person. It is also often synonymous with **good fortune.**

m **aelstrom** (1682), from Dutch **maelstroom,** "grinding stream," is a large and violent whirlpool or a chaotic state of affairs. In 1560, it was used to designate a notorious whirlpool off the northwest coast of Norway in the Arctic Ocean, the Maelstrom, which was reputed to swallow up all ships within a wide radius. This use of Maelstrom as a proper name is due to various Dutch maps, especially those in Mercator's legendary *Atlas* of 1595.

o **nslaught** (1625), a vigorous assault or attack, comes from Dutch **aanslag,** "a striking."

p **ickle** (1440), from Middle Dutch **pekel,** "brine, pickle," is a cucumber that has been preserved in brine or vinegar. Since 1562, the word has also been used informally of difficult or awkward situations.

p **it** (1841), the stone of a fruit, as of a peach, plum, or cherry, comes from Dutch **pit,** "kernel, pip," and is not related to **pit,** a hole in the ground.

p **lug** (1627), from Dutch **plugge,** "stopper, plug," is a piece of wood, rubber, or other solid material used to stop up a hole or to act as a wedge. It also signifies a piece of tobacco pressed into a flat cake cut off for chewing, especially by baseball players. It is used, too, of a device that makes an electrical connection to a circuit by insertion into a jack or receptacle of electrical equipment.

p **oll** (1209), from Dutch **polle,** "head, top of the head," once meant in English exactly what it meant in Dutch, that is, "the head of a man or animal." By Shakespeare's time, it referred to the number of people in any group, as ascertained by counting heads. Now, it signifies the casting or recording of votes at an election, the place where votes are cast, and the sampling or collection of opinions on a subject for the purpose of analysis.

poppycock (1865), nonsense, humbug, empty talk, comes from Dutch **pappekak,** "soft dung," a Dutch compound word equivalent to **pappe,** "pap, soft food for infants," and **kak,** "dung, excrement."

rack (c. 1305) comes from Middle Dutch **rec,** "bar, pole, shelf, framework," itself probably from the verb **recken,** "to reach, to stretch." In English, the word has several meanings. It is a framework of bars, wires, and pegs on which articles, such as clothes, kitchen utensils, and luggage, are arranged or deposited. It is sometimes a fixture with several tiered shelves for holding books. For pool players, a rack is a triangular wooden frame used to set up balls before playing. A rack was also an instrument of torture consisting of a framework on which the victim was tied by the wrists and ankles and stretched.

rant (1598), to talk in an extravagant or wild manner, to rave, comes from Dutch **ranten** or **randen,** "to talk foolishly," and first appears in English in Shakespeare's *Merry Wives of Windsor* and, four years later, in *Hamlet.*

rover (1390), from Middle Dutch **rover,** "robber," is a pirate.

rumple (1603), to wrinkle, crease, or crumple, is borrowed from the Dutch verb **rompelen,** "to wrinkle," or noun **rompel,** "a wrinkle."

Scone (1513), a small, rich biscuitlike quick bread made of wheat flour, oatmeal, or barley meal cooked on a griddle or baked on a sheet, is a shortened form of Dutch **schoonbrot,** "fine or white bread." One of the most intriguing passages involving scones can be found in Robert Louis Stevenson's novel *Kidnapped*: "We lay on the bare top of a rock, like scones upon a girdle." There is, moreover, an Australian slang expression "to go (someone) scone-hot," which means "to reprimand (someone) severely, to lose one's temper at (someone)."

Scoop (c. 1330), a ladlelike utensil, especially a deep shovel with a short handle, for taking up flour and sugar, or a hemispherical implement for dishing out ice cream or other soft foods, is borrowed from Middle Dutch **schope,** "bucket of a waterwheel, vessel for bailing out water."

Scow (1669), from Dutch **schouw,** "ferry boat or punt boat, boat propelled by a pole," is a large flat-bottomed vessel, such as a barge, punt, or rowboat.

Scrod (1841), a young codfish or haddock that is split for frying, boiling, baking, or broiling, is borrowed from Dutch **schrood** (from Middle Dutch **schrode,** meaning "piece cut off").

Sketch (1668), a rough drawing of something that gives the essential features without the details, a brief outline of facts, or a short theatrical piece, comes from Dutch **schets,** which itself was borrowed from Italian **schizzo** (from the Italian verb **schizzare,** "to splash").

Skipper (1390), from Middle Dutch **schipper,** "ship man," is the master or captain of a small merchant, fishing, or pleasure boat.

S**leigh** (1703), a sled, a vehicle on runners used to transport people or goods over snow or ice, comes from Dutch **slee,** contracted from **slede,** "sled."

S**loop** (1629), a small, single-masted sailing vessel, is borrowed from Dutch **sloep,** which may be related to the Old English verb **slupan,** "to glide," or may have come from Middle French **chaloupe,** "shallop."

S**muggle** (1687), to import or export goods surreptitiously contrary to the law and usually without paying duties imposed by the law, or simply to bring in or take something secretly, comes from Dutch **smokkelen** or Low German **smuggeln.**

S**nack** (1757), a light meal eaten between regular meals, comes from Middle Dutch **snack,** "a snap, a bite," related to the verb **snacken,** "to snap, to bite." The word is actually found in English as early as 1402, where it signifies "the bite of an animal, especially a dog."

S**nip** (1558), to cut up or off with a small, quick stroke or strokes, especially with scissors or some similar cutting instrument, comes from Dutch **snippen,** "to snatch, catch, clip." The noun **snip,** from the Dutch noun **snip,** meaning "a small piece of cloth that has been cut off," is found in English about thirty years before the verb.

S**noop** (1832), to prowl or pry, especially in a sneaky way, comes from Dutch **snoepen,** "to take and eat food on the sly." The word, which originally signified the consuming of dainties in a clandestine manner, has lost all reference to food. As a noun, it can be used of either amateur busybodies or professional private detectives.

Snuff (1671), to draw in (usually powdered tobacco) through the nose by inhaling, comes from Middle Dutch **snuf** or **snof,** "scent (of a thing), snuffling cold in the head, a sniffling." The word **snuff** is used in English as both a verb and a noun, the noun signifying either the powdered tobacco taken into the nostrils or ground tobacco placed between the cheek and gums. The practice of inhaling snuff appears to have become fashionable at the end of the seventeenth century, especially in Ireland and Scotland.

Span (1769), a pair of mules, horses, or other animals, especially a pair as nearly alike in size and color as possible, harnessed and driven together, is borrowed from Dutch **span,** "team (of oxen, horses)," related to the verb **spannen,** "to unite, to fasten." This **span** is not related to the span that indicates a unit of length or the distance between two objects.

Splint(er) (c. 1350), from Middle Dutch **splinte(r),** "metal plate, pin," refers to a rough piece, chip, or fragment of wood, bone, or stone that has been split or broken off from the main body. It was first used in English to indicate the plates or strips of overlapping metal that went into the making of medieval armor, as well as slender, flexible strips of wood suitable for interweaving in baskets.

Spook (1801), a ghost or specter, comes from Dutch **spook** and was a word borrowed in the United States from Dutch before it was ever used in Great Britain. There is a related German word, **Spuk,** which means "ghost, apparition, phantom, uproar, or mischief."

Stipple (1669), to paint, draw, or engrave with dots or small spots, sometimes in order to produce even or softly graded shadows, is borrowed from Dutch **stippelen,** "to dot," which is related to the Dutch noun **stip,** "a dot, a point."

Stoker (1660), a person who tends and fuels a furnace, especially a steam boiler on a ship, is derived from Dutch **stoker,** "one who stocks or feeds a fire."

Stoop (1789), a small platform, often uncovered, before the entrance of a house and approached by steps, was borrowed by Americans from Dutch **stoep.** It is not related to the English **stoop** that means "to bend the head and shoulders forward."

tattoo (1627), a signal on a drum, bugle, or trumpet at night for soldiers to repair to their quarters, comes from Dutch **taptoe,** "the tap [of a cask] is shut"—in other words, "no more drinking, time to go to bed." The word also indicates a rapid rhythmic rapping, as the sound of a frightened person's heartbeat. It is not related to the **tattoo** (borrowed from Tahitian) that is a pattern or picture made on the skin.

Waffle (1744), a kind of batter cake, with a gridlike pattern of indentations, eaten hot with butter, molasses, maple syrup, or, more recently, ice cream, is borrowed from Dutch **wafel,** "waffle, wafer," which, in turn, may be derived from a word related to the modern German **Wabe,** "honeycomb" because of the gridlike design.

Wagon (1511), a four-wheeled vehicle designed to transport anything from a young child to heavy loads, comes from Dutch **wagen,** the most general term for a wheeled vehicle. The Wagon, also called Charles's Wain, is another name for the constellation Ursa Major (or the Big Dipper).

Wainscot (c. 1352), wood, usually oak, used chiefly for fine panel-work, comes from Middle Dutch **wagenschot.** The **wagen** part of **wagenschot** means "a wheeled vehicle," but the **schot** element is obscure.

Walrus (1728), from Dutch **walrus,** "whale horse," which itself was derived from a Scandinavian word such as Danish or Norwegian **hvalros,** is a large marine mammal related to seals and sea lions, with flippers, a tough wrinkled skin, and two large tusks.

yacht (1557), a light fast-sailing ship used for private cruising, pleasure excursions, racing, or other noncommercial purposes, is borrowed from Dutch **yaght,** a shortened form of **yaght-schip,** "hunting ship."

yawl (1670), a small boat, as, for example, a small sailboat or fishing boat, is borrowed from Dutch **jol,** a general word for boat that originally may have meant "a Jutland boat."

Eskimo

anorak (1924), a weatherproof hooded pullover jacket that was originally made of fur and worn by Eskimos in arctic regions, is borrowed from Inuit (Greenlandic) **annoraaq.**

kayak (1757), from Inuit **qayaq,** is a light-framed Eskimo canoe covered with sealskins with a small opening in the center for the single occupant, who propels the craft by means of a double-bladed paddle. Kayaks are now made commercially from a variety of materials and used in sports.

mukluk, also spelled **muckluck** (1868), is a soft high boot made of sealskin, reindeer skin, or canvas, usually lined with fur, once worn solely by Eskimos but now designed for comfortable lounging about the house in the United States. The word is borrowed from Yupik **maklak,** "bearded seal," which was incorrectly assumed to mean "sealskin" and transferred to boots made of sealskin.

parka (1780), a hooded outer garment made of skins or fur worn by Eskimos in arctic regions or a similar jacket, usually made of windproof, water-repellent fabric for use by mountaineers, skiers, hunters, and the military, is borrowed from Aleut or Yupik **parka,** "skin, outer wear," itself from Russian **parka,** "pelt, skin jacket," and ultimately from Yurak.

Finnish

sauna (1881), from Finnish **sauna,** is a steambath that uses dry heat to induce perspiration, the steam being produced by pouring water on hot stones. The word is also applied to the room, generally made of wood, in which the steambath is taken.

French

adroit (1652), nimble in the use of the hands or body, bodily or mentally resourceful, clever or ingenious, comes from French **adroit,** "skillful," a combination of **a-,** "with, according to," and **droit,** "straight, correct."

a **mbience** (1889), also spelled **ambiance,** comes from French ambiance, "surrounding," which, in turn, was derived from Latin **ambire,** "to go around." It signifies the mood, character, feeling, tone, or atmosphere of a particular place (as of a restaurant) or milieu.

a **mbulance** (1809), from French **(hôpital) ambul(ant),** "walking hospital," seems to have come into general use during the Crimean War as a traveling hospital that followed an army in its movement, so as to give the swiftest possible aid to the wounded. By 1922, the word was being applied to a specially equipped vehicle for carrying sick or injured persons, usually to a hospital.

a **ntique** (1530), from French **antique** (from Latin **antiquus,** "in front, existing earlier, ancient"), as an adjective, means "belonging to the past." As a noun, it is used of a work of art, piece of furniture or china, or of any decorative object produced in an earlier period—according to various customs laws, at least one hundred years before the date of purchase.

a **ppliqué** (1841), from the French meaning "applied, fastened to," is a cutout design that is sewn onto a larger piece of material. The term is also used of metalwork.

a **rabesque** (1611), a flowing, spiraling, undulating, or serpentine line or motif, an ornament or style in which flowers, fruits, foliage, and sometimes animals and figures are represented in fancifully intertwined patterns, comes into English from French **arabesque,** which was borrowed from Italian **arabesco,** "Arabian." Since the 1830s, the word has also been applied to a pose in ballet in which the body of the dancer is bent forward from the hip on one leg with the corresponding arm extended in front and the other arm and leg behind.

attaché (1835), a diplomatic official attached to the suite of an ambassador or legation or a military officer assigned to a diplomatic post in a foreign nation in order to acquire military information, comes from a French past participle meaning "attached." **Attaché** is also used of a thin briefcase used especially to carry business papers or important documents.

avalanche (1789), a large mass of snow, ice, or rock detached from a mountain slope that rushes swiftly downward, is borrowed from French **avalanche,** from the Savoy dialect **avalance,** "descent," altered by association with **avaler,** "to descend rapidly," which may ultimately come from Latin **labina,** "landslide." Most scholars reject any connections, however tempting, to the word **lavare,** "to wash."

avant-garde (1910), from French **avant-garde,** "fore-guard," is a term applied to the pioneers or innovators, often unorthodox, radical, and daring, in any field, but especially in the visual, musical, or literary arts. Actually, the word was commonly used in English from 1470 to 1800 to signify the vanguard of an army.

avenue (1600), a wide street or a means of access, comes from French **avenue,** "approach," a participial form of the verb **avenir,** "to approach, to come to."

ballad (1385) first appears in English in Chaucer's *Legend of Good Women.* Derived from French **balade,** "dancing song" (from Old Provençal **balada,** "dance, dancing song"), a ballad is a popular song, frequently slow, romantic, and sentimental, or a narrative poem in rhythmic verse suitable for singing.

ballet (1667), is borrowed from French **ballet,** "little dance," the diminutive of French **bal,** "dance." It is the name applied to a classical dance characterized by elegance and precision, formalized steps, gestures, leaps, and turns to create expression and to tell a story.

baroque (1765), from French **baroque** (from Portuguese **barroco,** "rough or imperfectly shaped pearl" or "rocky, mountainous country"), is the term given to a florid style of art and architecture that began in Italy in the late Renaissance. The baroque is characterized by dramatic effects, elaborate and often grotesque ornamentation, and bizarre imagery. The word is also used of music written between 1600 and 1750. As an adjective, it means "extravagantly ornate or convoluted."

barrette (1901), from the French meaning "a little bar or rod," is a clip or clasp for holding a woman's or girl's hair in place.

barricade (1592), a defensive barrier hastily constructed to check the advance of an enemy or any obstacle that obstructs passage, is borrowed from French **barricade,** which came from the word **barrique,** meaning "barrel, hoghead," since the first street barricades in Paris were composed of casks filled with earth and paving stones. There is a day in French history (in 1588) called the Day of the Barricades, on which the judges of Chastellet sentenced various men to hanging. In 1611, Shakespeare used the word figuratively in *The Winter's Tale*, having Leontes say, "No Barricado for a Belly."

beau (1687), a lover, sweetheart, or suitor, a male escort for a woman, comes from the French adjective meaning "handsome, beautiful, or fine."

beef (1300), the flesh of an ox, bull, or cow, is borrowed from Old French **buef,** "ox, cow." The modern French word for cow, **boeuf,** is similar.

beige (1858), a very light brown or yellowish gray color, is borrowed from French **beige.** The word is used, too, of cloth made of natural, undyed wool.

belle (1622), a young woman admired for her charm and beauty, comes from the French adjective **belle,** "beautiful, fair, fine, good-looking."

bigot (1661), a person who is intolerant of other people's opinions, beliefs, or creed, is borrowed from Middle French **bigot,** a derogatory name applied by the French to the Normans. Interestingly, just as the English language borrowed the word from French, the French language had originally borrowed the word from Old English **bi God,** "by God." In the sixteenth century, the word **bigot** was also used of any hypocritical adherent of religion.

biscuit (1330), shortened from Middle French **pain biscuit,** "twice-cooked bread," is used of a kind of crisp, dry bread made into small cakes, raised with baking powder, baking soda, or yeast. It is also the name given to porcelain or earthenware after the first firing and before being glazed or painted. The literal meaning, "twice-cooked," points to the original mode of preparation. The word **bisque** (1664), which is short for **biscuit,** is used of vitreous china that is left unglazed and is a light pinkish tan.

bizarre (1648), unusual in appearance, extravagantly strange, odd, fantastic, comes from French **bizarre,** which, in turn, may come from either Spanish **bizarro,** "handsome, brave," or Italian **bizzarro,** "lively, capricious, eccentric." Some have suggested that the Spanish word is an adaptation of Basque **bizarra,** "beard," since **hombre de bigote,** "mustached man," is used in Spanish to signify a "man of spirit."

blanket (1346), from Old French **blankete,** "little white thing," was formed from the French adjective **blanc,** "white." Originally, blankets were white or undyed woolen stuff used for clothing, but the word is now applied to any large, rectangular piece of soft fabric used for warmth, as a bed covering, or as a covering for animals such as horses and dogs. The word is often used figuratively, as in **a blanket of snow,** as well as in such expressions as **wet blanket,** to indicate a person who dampens enthusiasm or pleasure (as a wet blanket smothers a fire), and **born on the wrong side of the blanket,** to indicate that someone is illegitimate.

blasé (1819), bored with life, wearied, as if by too much worldly pleasure, is borrowed from the French past participle of **blaser,** "to exhaust, cloy, sicken from excess."

blouse (1828), a usually light, loose-fitting garment, generally worn by women and children, that covers the body from the neck to the waist and is usually tucked inside a skirt or pants, is probably borrowed from the phrase **vêtement de laine blouse,** "garment of short (uncarded, pure) wool."

bonbon (1796), a piece of candy, a lozenge made of sugar, a fondant or chocolate containing fruit, nuts, or a fondant center, is borrowed from **bonbon,** "good-good," which was originally a repetitive compound word used in the nursery by adults speaking to little children.

boudoir (1781), a woman's bedroom or private sitting room, usually elegantly furnished, where she may retire to be alone, comes from French **boudoir,** which means "a sulking place." Related to the verb **bouder,** "to sulk, to pout," a boudoir was presumably where a woman would go to wear a sullen expression or thrust out her lips in displeasure. In the eighteenth century, the word sometimes also referred to a man's den or study.

bouffant (1880), from French "swelling" (the present participle of the verb **bouffer,** "to swell"), is a woman's hairstyle in which the hair is teased to give it a fluffy or puffed-out appearance. The bouffant became stylish and elegant in the early 1960s in America when First Lady Jacqueline Kennedy, assisted by her ubiquitous hairdresser, Kenneth, donned the sculpturally rounded hairstyle like a crown. The trend had actually begun in the late 1950s when *Life* magazine published pictures of women in bouffants magnificently adorned with jewels and feathers. In 1958, the models of French designer Givenchy wore chic full-headed bouffants that degenerated, within the year, into such stiffened, lacquered caricatures as the bubble and beehive.

boulevard (1769), a wide, sometimes landscaped avenue or thoroughfare in a city, is borrowed from French **boulevard,** a corruption of a Picard or Walloon word meaning "rampart or avenue built on the site of a demolished rampart." The French word originally meant the horizontal portion of a rampart, the promenade built on a razed fortification. The word **boulevard** is etymologically related to another English word: **bulwark.**

bouquet (1716), a nosegay or bunch of flowers, is borrowed from French **bouquet,** "bunch." From Old French **bosquet,** it originally meant a thicket or grove, a little forest. **Bouquet** is also applied to the characteristic scent, aroma, or fragrance of wines and liqueurs.

bourgeois (1564), a member of the middle class, comes ultimately from Old French **borjois,** which is related to the German word **burg,** "city." A bourgeois was a solid citizen who, like a burgher, lived in a town or borough and achieved success (property and respectability) as a merchant or shopkeeper. The word is used disparagingly of capitalists (viewed as parasitic exploiters of the proletariat) in socialist and communist literature, as, for example, the writings of Marx and Engels. **Bourgeoisie** (1707) signifies the bourgeois class.

boutique (1767), from French **boutique,** "shop," is a small, exclusive fashion shop or department within a larger store, especially one that specializes in trend-setting clothes designed by a couturier.

boutonniere (1877), from the French word meaning "buttonhole," is a flower or small spray of flowers worn, usually by a man, in the buttonhole of a lapel.

braise (1769), from French **braiser,** "to cook on live coals," means "to cook or stew meat, fish, or vegetables by sauteeing in fat (or oil) and then simmering in a tightly closed pan in very little liquid."

brassiere (1911), a woman's close-fitting undergarment used to support the breasts, is borrowed from French **brassière,** "bodice." The word, which originally meant "arm protector" or "article for the arm (**bras**)," is etymologically related to the English word **bracelet.** In his 1961 novel *Catch-22*, Joseph Heller wrote one of his most oft-quoted lines: "An unhooked brassiere was as close as you ever hoped to get to Paradise."

brazier (1690), a large, flat pan (or metal receptacle) for holding live coals and used to heat a room, comes from French **braise,** "live coals," and is related to the English word **braise.** The word **brazier** is also used of cooking devices that hold live coals covered by wire grills upon which meat is placed.

bric-a-brac (1840) is the name given to various small articles of sentimental or decorative value, as, for example, china, plates, statuettes, and fans—a word synonymous with trinkets, gewgaws, and knickknacks. Borrowed from French **bric-à-brac,** "at random, by hook or by crook, without rhyme or reason," the word seems to have been first used in English in 1840 by the novelist William Thackeray, when he complained in his *Paris Sketch Book* that "the palace of Versailles has been turned into a bricabrac shop."

briquette (1883), from French "little brick," has been used, since the nineteenth century, to signify small blocks of compressed coal dust or charcoal used for fuel and, more recently, for barbecuing. In the 1920s, the word began to be applied to small blocks of ice cream, as well.

brochure (1765), a small pamphlet or booklet, especially one that contains descriptive or advertising material, is borrowed from French **brochure,** "a stitched work" (formed from the verb **brocher,** "to stitch").

brouhaha (1890), a commotion, uproar, hubbub, hullabaloo, comes from French **brou, ha ha!,** an exclamation used by characters playing the devil in sixteenth-century French dramas. This expression is no doubt a distortion of the Hebrew phrase (from the 118th psalm) **barukh habba (beshem adhonai)** "blessed is he who comes (in the name of the Lord)." Brouhaha is similar, in many ways, to another English expression, **hocus pocus,** which is applied to meaningless chants used in conjuring or incantations, as well as to needlessly mysterious activity or talk that is employed to conceal a deception. Like **brouhaha, hocus pocus** is a distorted alteration of a phrase in a foreign language, namely, the Latin words **hoc est corpus [meum]** "this is [my] body," which is the Eucharistic formula once used by Roman Catholic priests during the Mass at the moment when worshipers believed that a piece of bread was being changed into the body of Jesus Christ. **Hocus pocus** was used as a pseudo-Latin rhyming phrase by jugglers and magicians.

brunette (1712), from French "little brown (woman)," is a word applied to women with dark hair, dark eyes, and an olive complexion. It sometimes simply means "dark-haired." The word **brunet,** used of men, is less common in English.

buccaneer (1661), from French **boucanier,** "one who hunts wild oxen, bull hunter" or "one who dries meat on a barbecue," is the name given to any of the freebooters, pirates, or rovers who preyed on Spanish ships and colonies, especially in the West Indies, in the second half of the seventeenth century. The name was first used in English of the French hunters of St. Domingo who dried and smoked flesh on **boucans,** or barbecues, in the manner of the native Americans.

buffet (1718), from French **buffet,** is a sideboard or cabinet for holding table linens and china, as well as a meal set out on a table so that guests may serve themselves.

bulletin (1651), a brief account issued to inform the public of something, specifically, a news item broadcast over radio or television, comes from French **bulletin,** itself from Old French **bullette,** the diminutive of **bulle,** "papal edict" (from Latin **bulla,** "sealed document, official seal"). The earliest bulletins, then, were issued by the pope. The word is used, too, of pamphlets and peri-odicals, whether of corporations and governmental agencies or of learned societies.

bureau (1720), from French "writing desk, office," can be an office or agency for collecting or distributing news or infor-mation, or it can be a chest of drawers, generally with a mirror on top. The French word **bureau,** before it meant desk, meant a kind of coarse woolen cloth that was used to cover desks; the word was derived from Latin **burra,** "wool, fluff, shaggy cloth."

burlesque (1656), from French **burlesque** (which was bor-rowed from Italian **burlesco,** "pertaining to a jest or pertain-ing to mockery"), is a literary or dramatic composition that aims at exciting laughter through ludicrous caricature and grotesque par-ody. In the United States, **burlesque** also signifies a provocative stage show with striptease acts, slapstick humor, vulgar skits, and coarse songs.

cabaret (1632), from French **cabaret,** "taproom," originally signified in English a wooden dwelling or shed. The current meaning of **cabaret**—a restaurant, nightclub, or cafe providing food, drink, music, and sometimes a floor show—may be found in English as early as 1655.

cabinet (1550), a piece of furniture with shelves and drawers for holding, displaying, or storing such items as curios, files, toiletries, kitchen utensils, and televisions, comes from Middle French **cabinet** (the diminutive of **cabin**), meaning "little hut" or "room on a ship." Actually, in the sixteenth century, the English word was used with the now obsolete meaning of "a soldier's tent" or "a rustic cottage."

C afe (1802), a small and informal coffeehouse or restaurant, sometimes with an enclosed section extending onto the sidewalk, is borrowed from the French **café,** "coffee." The word is sometimes used of barrooms and nightclubs.

C affeine (1830), a white, crystalline alkaloid found in the leaves and seeds of the coffee and tea plants, and from the nuts of the cola tree, comes from **caféine,** which is composed of **café,** the French word for "coffee," and the **-ine** suffix used in chemistry. Caffeine was discovered in coffee by Runge in 1820. Seven years later, Oudry found a crystalline substance in tea, which he called **theine,** since he believed that it was a distinct compound. When Jobat proved that it was identical with caffeine, the word **theine** was abandoned.

C aisson (1704), from French **caisson,** "box, large chest, locker, bunker," is the name given to chests and two-wheeled wagons used for carrying explosives and artillery ammunition, to watertight structures (cofferdams) used in laying the underwater foundations of bridges, and to floats used to raise sunken vessels.

C alorie (1866), a unit of heat or the amount of food having the energy-producing value of one kilocalorie or large calorie, comes from French **calorie** (from Latin **calor,** "heat"). The word **calorie** was not in general English use before 1880.

C amaraderie (1840), from French **camaraderie,** means comradeship, fellowship, the loyalty and familiarity that exists between good friends. During the Civil War, Sir William Howard Russell, an Englishman visiting the United States, wrote in *My Diary North and South:* "The only camaraderie I have witnessed in America exists among the West Point men."

Camisole (1848), from French "vest," is a short negligee jacket, often trimmed with lace, worn by women or a short sleeveless garment worn beneath a thin, transparent bodice.

Camouflage (1917), the disguising of military equipment to deceive an enemy, as by painting objects or screening them with nets and foliage until they blend into the background, comes from French **camouflage,** formed from the verb **camoufler,** "to disguise," which, in turn, is related to **camouflet,** "smoke blown in someone's face as a practical joke." **Camouflet** was contracted from **chault moufflet,** "hot puff, hot breath." Today, the word **camouflet** is used of underground explosions of bombs or mines that do not break the surface, but instead leave cavities filled with gas and smoke, to suffocate or cut off the retreat of an enemy. **Camouflage** is applied to clothing with a mottled design, generally green and brown, used in military activities.

Campaign (1647), borrowed from French **campagne,** "field, open countryside," denotes a systematic course of aggressive activities designed to bring about a specific result, as, for example, military, sales, and election campaigns. The word first appeared as a military term. Throughout the history of the West, most armies engaged in warfare remained in towns, garrisons, and camps during the winter, and came forth into the open country at the first approach of summer. They "took the field" (French **campagne**). "To be in the field" became synonymous with the various military operations performed during this time.

Canapé (1890), a thin piece of bread or toast on which cheese, caviar, anchovies, or other savories are spread, is borrowed from French **canapé,** "a covering or netting, originally for a bed." Hence, a canapé is related etymologically to a canopy. Both words are descendants of Medieval Latin **canopeum,** "a mosquito net," which was borrowed, in turn, from Greek **konopeion,** "a bed with netting to keep off gnats." The earliest citation of canapé in English may be found in *Mrs. Beeton's Cookery Book* (1890), where she speaks of anchovy canapés.

C**anard** (c. 1850), a false or unfounded rumor or report, especially a fabricated derogatory story, comes from French **canard,** "duck." Most scholars agree that the English use of **canard** as an absurd story circulated to capitalize on people's gullibility comes from an old French expression, **vendre un canard à moitié,** "to half-sell a duck." Since half-selling a duck is not selling the duck at all, the expression meant "to take in, make a fool of" and eventually changed into the noun **canard.**

C**aprice** (1667), a sudden, unpredictable, seemingly unmotivated change of mind (or weather), a whim, comes from French **caprice** (from Italian **capriccio,** "a head with hair standing on end," formed from **capo,** "head," and **riccio,** "hedgehog"). Thus, the word **caprice** has evolved from the spiky, bristly head of a hedgehog to a human head with its hair standing on end (in amazement or fear) to the cause of such amazement—an impulsive action.

C**aramel** (1725), a kind of chewy candy or a liquid made from heating sugar, the liquid used for coloring and flavoring food, comes from French **caramel.** The origin of the French word is obscure. Some have suggested that it is derived from Latin **calamellus,** "little reed," which was initially confused with **canna mellis,** "sugar or honey cane."

C**arbine** (1605), a short rifle used in the cavalry or a light semi-automatic rifle, comes from French **carabine,** the name given to the small weapon carried by a **carabin,** a lightly armed cavalryman. **Carabin** may have developed from French **(e)scarabin,** the term applied to gravediggers for plague victims, who were themselves named after the **escarbot,** the dung beetle or scarab, which rolls balls of dung in which it lays its eggs.

Caress (1611), from French **caresse** (from the verb **caresser,** "to fondle") and ultimately from Latin **carus,** "dear, beloved," is an act or gesture expressing affection, be it an embrace, a kiss, or, usually, a gentle touching.

Carrot (1533), a plant of the parsley family cultivated for its nutritious tapering orange root, eaten raw or cooked, comes from French **carotte.** Today, **carrot** is also used for an incentive or promised reward.

Cashier (1596), from Middle French **caissier,** "custodian of a money-box, treasurer," is one who collects payments for purchases or keeps records of financial transactions. The French word **caissier** evolved from Latin **capsarius,** the name given to a slave boy in an ancient Roman household who had to carry the schoolbooks of his youthful master.

Casserole (1706), from French **casserole,** "ladlelike pan," denotes both a baking dish of glass or porcelain, often with a cover, and any food cooked and served in such a dish.

Cassette (1793), from French "little box, little case," is a flat case or container that holds magnetic tape and film or plates for use in a camera. Back in 1793, it signified a small box or chest for jewels or letters.

C **handelier** (1736), from the French meaning "something that holds candles," is a decorative branched light fixture usually hung from the roof or ceiling.

C **haperon(e)** (1720), a person, most often a married or older woman, who, for the sake of propriety, accompanies a young unmarried woman in public, is borrowed from French **chaperon,** "hood" (from Middle French "cowl, head covering"). The hood was originally worn by noblemen (it was part of the full dress of Knights of the Garter), but after the sixteenth century, it was donned by ladies, many of whom would be called to serve as guides and guardians of young women's virtue. Today, **chaperone** is used of any adult present at a school dance or social function to preserve order and propriety among the young people.

C **harade** (1776), from French **charade** (from Provençal **char-rad[o],** "entertainment," from **charr[a],** "chatter, babble") is a game in which players, divided into two teams, take turns acting out in pantomime words, phrases, or movie and play titles, which the other members of their team try to guess. It is also a deceptive act or blatant pretense. The word, which started out meaning "rapid, incessant language" in Provençal, now has added to it an element of silence.

C **hassis** (1655), from French **chassis,** "frame," is the name given to the frame and working parts of an automobile or to the main landing gear of an airplane. In the seventeenth century, the word referred to a window frame lined with paper, linen, or glass. In the nineteenth century, the word signified the lower part of the carriage of a barbette or casemate gun. Its current meaning first appeared in English print in 1903.

Chauffeur (1899), a person employed to drive a private auto-mobile or limousine, comes from the French word meaning "stoker" or "he who heats, he who warms up." Before they drove their owners' cars, the first chauffeurs in France had to heat up the engine until a head of steam powerful enough to move the vehicle was built up.

Chef (1842), a skilled cook who presides over the kitchen of a restaurant or hotel, planning menus, overseeing the prepara-tion of food, and supervising the staff, comes from French **chef,** "head," which is short for **chef de cuisine,** "head of (the) kitchen."

Chenille (1738), from French **chenille,** "(hairy) caterpillar," is used of any fabric, especially wool, cotton, silk, or rayon, with a pile that protrudes like the hairs of a caterpillar. It is also applied to velvety cord or yarn of silk or worsted used in embroidery, trim-ming, and fringes. The earliest use of the word in English appears in 1738 in a description of a certain Lady Huntingdon's petticoat, which "was black velvet embroidered with chenille."

Chic (1856), from French **chic,** "stylish, natty," means exactly the same in English—attractive and stylish. As a noun, it signifies a kind of style and elegance in dress (and mind-set). It is sometimes argued that **chic** originated as an abbreviation of **chicane,** "to be subtle or crafty, to employ tricks." Others suggest that the French language borrowed it from German **Schick,** "skill, tact."

Chiffon (1765), a diaphanous plain-woven fabric of silk, nylon, or rayon, or the decorative adjuncts of a woman's dress (such as ribbon or lace), comes from French **chiffon,** "rag, scrap, bit of stuff." In the late 1920s, the word became an English cooking term referring to the light, frothy filling of certain pies and cakes con-taining beaten egg whites or a gelatin mixture.

Chowder (1732), a thick soup or stew made of clams, fish, or mussels, with potatoes, tomatoes, onions, and other ingredients, comes from Frence **chaudière**, "kettle, pot." In the fishing villages of Brittany in France, **faire la chaudière** means to fill a large pot with fish, biscuits, and other ingredients. The contents of this culinary hodgepodge are then cooked and distributed to all those who contributed to the stew. It is believed that the Breton fishermen carried the custom to Newfoundland, long renowned for its chowder, and from Canada, it eventually spread to New England.

Chute (1725), an inclined plane for conveying water, grain, coal, laundry, and other objects to a lower level, is borrowed from French **chute**, "fall, drop." **Chute** is also the name given to a water slide in an amusement park. The word **parachute** is a compound of **para**, "guard against," and **chute**, "fall." And **chute-the-chute**, synonymous with **roller coaster**, an elevated railway with sharp curves and steep dips at a carnival or amusement park, entered the English language in the 1890s.

Cigarette (1842), from French "little cigar," is a slender roll of finely cut tobacco meant to be smoked. Cigarettes were a New World invention. Spanish explorers, who found the Aztecs smoking them, brought them back to Spain, Portugal, and other Mediterranean countries. Cigarettes did not, however, become popular in northern Europe until the 1850s, when British soldiers carried them home from the Crimean War. By the end of the Civil War, in 1865, the cigarette had arrived in the United States.

Clairvoyance (1847), a supposed power or faculty attributed to certain persons of seeing and having insights into objects beyond the range of ordinary perception, comes from French **clair-voyance**, "clear-sightedness." The usual laboratory test of clair-voyance is card guessing. The eighteenth-century Swedish philosopher and theologian Emanuel Swedenborg demonstrated his unique extrasensory abilities when he described a huge fire that was burning in Stockholm, more than three hundred miles away from Göteborg, where he was residing.

Claque (1864), an organized group of hired applauders in a theater or any group of sycophants ready to applaud their leader, comes from French **claque,** "a smack, a clap of the hand."

Claret (c. 1396), a red table wine originally produced in Bordeaux but now made in other places as well, comes from Middle French **claret,** which was short for **vin claret** "wine (made) clear."

Clarinet (1796), a single-reed woodwind instrument having a cylindrical tube with a bell-shaped orifice, is borrowed from French **clarinette,** "little clear-sounding instrument." The clarinet was invented in the seventeenth century, probably by Johann Denner (1655–1707), a German flute maker. By assigning the clarinet a regular seat in a symphonic orchestra and composing several magnificent solo pieces for it, Mozart elevated the status of the instrument.

Clef (1579), the symbol placed at the beginning of a musical staff to indicate the name and pitch corresponding to its lines and spaces, comes from Middle French **clef,** "key." There are three clefs in use, the C, tenor, or alto, clef; the G, or treble, clef; and the F, or bass, clef.

Cliché (1832) comes from French **cliché,** "stereotype or electrolyte plate, stencil," a noun use of the past participle of the verb **clicher,** "to make such a plate, to stereotype." The French verb **clicher** is thought to be onomatopoeic, an imitation of the sound made when the matrix is dropped into the molten metal to make a stereotype plate. In the 1830s, when **cliché** first came into the English language, it signified a stereotype block or the cast applied to a metal stereotype of a wood engraving to print from. By 1892, the word came to have its current meaning—a platitude; a trite, stereotyped expression; a hackneyed or commonplace plot, character, melody, or idea that has lost its freshness and force through long overuse. Among the more famous clichés: **busy as a bee, strong as an ox, bored to tears, sadder but wiser,** and **scared stiff.**

Clientele (1563), clients or customers considered as a group, comes from French **clientèle** (from Latin **clientela,** "a group of clients seeking the protection or influence of someone powerful"). In ancient Rome, clients were often poets and philosophers who lived under the patronage of a patrician. The English word **clientele** has a fascinating history. Commonly used in the sixteenth century, the word virtually disappeared in the seventeenth century. The obsolete word was then readopted by the French (and later by the English) in the middle of the nineteenth century, and has been in use ever since.

Clique (1711), a small, select group of people, an exclusive group of friends and associates, is borrowed from French **clique,** "clique, clicking sound," apparently a metaphorical use of Middle French **clique,** "latch," which was formed from the verb **cliquer,** "to click, to make noise, to resound." This suggests that early cliques were originally claques.

Coiffure (1631), a style or fashion of arranging the hair, comes from French **coiffure,** "headgear, style of hairdressing" (from the French verb **coiffer,** "to array the hair").

Collage (1919), a form of art in which newspaper clippings, parts of photographs, pieces of paper, string, theater tickets, fragments of an envelope, fabric, and wallpaper, among other objects, are placed in juxtaposition and glued to a single surface, is borrowed from French **collage,** "pasting, sticking, gluing" (formed from **colle,** "paste, glue"). The invention of the collage is frequently attributed to Pablo Picasso and Georges Braque, even though collage techniques existed in the nineteenth century. Some of the other great collage artists include Jean Arp, Max Ernst, Kurt Schwitters, and Robert Rauschenberg, and the Dadaists. Henri Matisse's **papiers découpés** were an adaptation of the collage technique.

Concierge (1646), the person in charge of the entrance or lobby of a building or apartment house (especially in France) who screens visitors, accepts deliveries for the tenants, serves as janitor, and controls the operation of the elevators, is borrowed from French **concierge,** "porter, doorkeeper."

Connoisseur (1714), one who is an expert, especially in the fine arts (such as painting and sculpture), or in matters of taste (for example, horses, wines, delicacies), and is able to act as a discerning judge, is borrowed from French **connoisseur,** "knower, judge."

Corduroy (1787), a kind of coarse, durable, thick-ribbed, generally cotton pile fabric, often worn by laborers, is assumed to come from French **cord du roy (roi),** "the king's cord." Since the fabric had no connection whatsoever with France and, more importantly, since no such name has ever been used in France, it is assumed that the word is an English invention. **Corduroy** is also applied to a road or bridge constructed of logs laid side by side transversely.

Corps (1711), an organized subdivision of a military organization (for example, the Marine Corps) or a group of people acting together (as the diplomatic corps or press corps), is borrowed from French **corps**, "body," which is an abbreviation of **corps d'armée**, "body of the army." The word appears to have come into the English language during the campaigns of John Churchill, the first duke of Marlborough (1650–1722).

Corset (1299), from Old French **corset**, "little body," was the name given to a close-fitting body garment worn as an outside garment in the Middle Ages. Since 1795, **corset** has signified a close-fitting undergarment, extending from above or below the bust or from the waist to below the hips, usually stiffened with whalebone and tightened by lacing, worn by women to shape and support their bodies.

Coterie (1738), a clique, an intimate and exclusive group of people, comes from French **coterie**, the word applied to an association of peasants or tenant farmers (and related to Medieval Latin **coterius**, "cottager, farm laborer"). Zoologists use the word today to denote a group of prairie dogs occupying a communal burrow.

Cotillion (1766), now a formal ball usually given for debutantes, was originally a lively eighteenth-century French social dance performed by couples and resembling a quadrille. **Cotillion** is borrowed from the French word meaning "petticoat," an object of apparel much in evidence at these dances.

Coupe (1834) is used of the end compartment in a European railway carriage, a short four-wheeled closed horse-drawn carriage with an inside seat for two passengers and an outside seat for the driver, and of a closed two-door automobile that is shorter than a sedan of the same model. The word is borrowed from French **coupe** or **coupé**, which is short for **carosse coupé** "shortened coach."

Crochet (1848), needlework done with a single thread and a needle having a small hook at one end for drawing the thread or yarn through intertwined loops, comes from French **crochet,** "little hook."

Croquet (1858), an outdoor game played by propelling wooden balls with wooden mallets through iron hoops or wickets set out on a lawn, is borrowed from French **croquet,** "little hook" (or "hockey stick"). Introduced into England in 1852, the game attained great popularity in the middle of the nineteenth century. It traveled to the United States about 1870.

Croupier (1731), an employee of a gambling casino who rakes in money or chips and assists at a gaming table, comes from French **croupier,** meaning "one who sits behind another person on horseback" (from the French **croupe,** "rump"). Originally, a croupier was a person who went halves with a card player or dice player and stood behind him to assist.

Cul-de-sac (1738), from French "bottom of the bag," was first used in English by doctors and anatomy students to describe any saclike vessel or pouch in the body, like the cecum. By the beginning of the nineteenth century, the word was used, as it is today, of streets or lanes closed at one end, of blind alleys and dead-end streets. More recently, the word has been applied to situations in which any further progress is impossible.

curfew (1285), a parental regulation establishing a specific time in the evening when children must be home, or a governmental or military order forbidding civilians or other groups of unauthorized persons to be outdoors after a stated hour, comes from Middle French **covrefeu,** "(it) covers (the) fire." The original purpose of the curfew seems to have been to prevent the large conflagrations that might arise from domestic fires left unattended at night. Indeed, during medieval times in Europe, a bell was rung at a fixed hour in the evening as a signal for covering or extinguishing fires. There is a story, unsupported by historical evidence, that can be traced back to the sixteenth century, claiming that the curfew was introduced into England by William the Conqueror at the end of the eleventh century as a measure of political repression.

dandelion (1513), a weed having edible toothed or notched leaves used in salads, many-rayed golden-yellow flowers occasionally used in wine making, and rounded clusters of white, fluffy seeds, is borrowed from Middle French **dent de lion,** "tooth of (a) lion," a reference to the toothed edges of the plant's leaves.

debacle (1802), a complete collapse or disaster, a total fiasco, a violent rout or downfall, or a tumultuous breaking up and sudden rush of ice in a river, is derived from French **débâcle** (from the verb **débâcler,** "to unbar, to clear").

debris (1708), the remains of something broken down or destroyed, ruins, trash, litter, comes from French **débris** (from the verb **debriser,** "to break down or into pieces"). The word is also used by geologists to signify an accumulation of fragments or rock.

debut (1751), the first public appearance on the stage, on television, in the movies, of an actor, actress, musician, or dancer, comes from French début (from the verb **débuter,** "to make the first stroke in a billiards game, to lead off the game"). The word also signifies a formal entrance into society, the first appearance of a new product on the market, or the beginning of a career. **Debutante** (1801), the feminine of the present participle of the French verb, is the name given to a young woman making her debut into society. Few debutantes, one may safely say, are aware of the poolroom metaphor that surrounds their entrance into society.

decor (1897), the style, decoration, or furnishings of a room or building, or the scenic decoration of a theater stage, comes from French **décor,** "decoration, set."

deluxe (1819), from French **de luxe,** "of luxury," is an adjective indicating that something is "elegant, sumptuous, of the highest quality, luxurious, or expensive."

demitasse (1842), from French "half cup," is either a small cup used for serving strong black coffee such as espresso or the actual contents of the cup.

dentist (1759), from French **dentiste,** "one who works with teeth," is a person whose profession involves treating diseases and malformations of the teeth and gums; removing, correcting, and replacing decayed, damaged, or lost parts of teeth; filling, crowning, straightening, and extracting teeth; and inserting artificial dentures. The first dentists were Egyptian, their profession dating as far back as 3700 B.C. The earliest recorded reference to a toothache is found on a Sumerian clay tablet, excavated in Ur, that dates to about 2500 B.C. The tablet, one of many medical tablets, contains medicines, surgical procedures, and various spells and incantations. It also contains the dubious scientific hypothesis that worms are the cause of tooth decay. Dentistry existed among the Chinese, the ancient Hindus, the Greeks, and the Romans. Hebrew priests with bad teeth were not allowed to conduct services in the Temple of

Jerusalem. During the eighteenth century, the French took the lead in the field of dentistry. Indeed, the man generally acknowledged to be the "father of modern dentistry," Pierre Fauchard, revolutionized dental surgery. In his work *The Surgeon Dentist*, published in 1728, he covered tooth decay, gum diseases, and medicines useful in treating both. He also invented the bandelette, a device for expanding crowded teeth. It was not until the middle of the nineteenth century that the United States surpassed France in the development of dentistry.

d **epot** (1798), a bus or railroad station, a storehouse or warehouse, a place where military stores are deposited, is borrowed from French **dépôt** (from Latin **depositum**, "something put down").

d **essert** (1600), the name given to cakes, pies, fruit, puddings, and ice cream when they are served after a dinner or supper, comes from French **dessert,** "removal of the dishes" (from the verb **desservir,** "to clear the table").

d **étente** (1908), an easing of tension or strained relations, especially in a political situation, by negotiations, is borrowed from French **détente,** "loosening, relaxation" (formed from the verb **détendre,** "to unbend, to slacken, to relax").

d **etour** (1738), a turning or deviation from the main route or the usual procedure, a roundabout or circuitous way of proceeding when the direct road is closed, comes from French **détour,** "turning off, dodge" (from the verb **détourner** "to divert, to turn away, to deflect").

deuce (1481), from Middle French **deus,** "two," is a card with two pips, a die with two spots, or a situation in tennis in which a player, tied with another, must score two successive points to win the game or two successive games to win the set. **Deuce** in tennis is an abbreviation of the phrase **à deux de jeu.**

discotheque (1954), an intimate nightclub where recorded (and sometimes live) music is played for dancing, is borrowed from French "disk archive, record library."

divorcée (1813), from French **divorcée,** means a divorced woman. The masculine equivalent, **divorcé,** is almost never used in English.

douche (1766), a jet or stream of water, sometimes containing a dissolved medicating or cleansing agent, directed toward some part of the body for hygienic reasons, comes from French **douche** (from Italian **doccia,** "water pipe, conduit pipe," from the Latin **ductio,** "a leading or conveying of water"). The word is also used of an instrument, such as a syringe, used to give a douche or of a cleansing with a douche.

echelon (1796), from French "rung of a ladder," is a formation of troops, ships, or airplanes with its units each somewhat to the left or right of the one in the rear like a series of steps. It also denotes a grade of command or authority.

éclair (1861), an oblong cream puff, filled with whipped cream or custard and often frosted with chocolate or icing, comes from French **éclair,** "lightning," as if the custard filling or whipped cream were shot through the pastry like a stroke of lightning.

e lite (1823), from French "chosen," denotes the best of anything considered collectively, especially a group or class of people. It sometimes refers to a group of powerful people exerting the strongest influence inside a larger group.

e nsemble (1750), from French "together," refers to a group or entity, all of whose members or parts are taken together, such as the united performance of an entire group of actors, dancers, singers, or musicians, or a group of supporting players, or the complete costume of a person, especially when all parts and accessories are in harmony.

e ntourage (1832), a group of attendants or associates, a retinue or following, is borrowed from French "setting, surrounding," formed from the verb **entourer,** "to surround, to hedge."

e ntrepreneur (1828), from French "one who undertakes (some task)," denotes a person who organizes, manages, and assumes the risks and responsibilities of an enterprise, especially a business.

e nvelope (1714), from the French word meaning "covering," formed from the verb **envelopper,** "to envelope, wrap (up), enfold, encase," signifies a flat paper container, as for a letter, a wrapper, or the bag containing the gas in an airship or balloon. Biologists apply the word to a surrounding or enclosing structure, such as a membrane, shell, corolla, or integument.

e nvoy (1643), a minister or diplomatic agent acting as a representative of the government in its dealing with another nation, comes from French **envoyé,** "someone sent," the past participle of **envoyer,** "to send."

etiquette (1750) is borrowed from French **etiquette** (from Middle French **estiquette,** "ticket, especially one belonging to a soldier, memorandum, label)." In English, the word denotes the conduct or social behavior prescribed for any class or community, as well as the code of ethical behavior established in any profession. Originally, **etiquette** signified the required code of usage in matters involving court ceremonies and formal rituals.

fabric (1483), borrowed from Middle French **fabrique,** "factory, mill, invention," was originally used in English to denote a structure or building. Later, the word was extended to include cloth made by weaving, knitting, or felting fibers and the pattern created by the arrangement of the crystal grains in a rock.

facade (1656), the face or front of a building, or a false or superficial appearance or the illusion of something, is borrowed from French **façade,** "front," which was derived, via Upper Italian **faciada,** from Italian **facciata** (from **faccia,** "face").

farce (1530), from Middle French **farce,** "stuffing, forcemeat" (from the verb **farcir,** "to stuff, to cram"), is a light, humorous dramatic work characterized by broad satire and an improbable plot, rather than by the development of character. The verb **farce,** now obsolete, meant "to stuff," as in the instructions of a fourteenth-century cookbook: "farce the cattle as you farce a goose." The verb was used as a culinary term in the fifteenth and sixteenth centuries (for example, "a pig farced with sage"), and in 1736, they were still farcing cucumbers. **Farceur** (1781), an actor or writer of farces, comes from French **farceur. Farci** (1903) has reappeared in its French form as a cooking term that means "stuffed," especially with oysters or mushrooms, as in **eggs farcis.**

femme fatale (1912), from French "deadly woman," is the term applied to a dangerously attractive woman, especially one who lures men into compromising situations. The **femme fatale** has been among the stereotypes most cherished by movie audiences everywhere and includes steamy performances by Lana Turner in *The Postman Always Rings Twice,* Jessica Lange in a remake of the same movie, Barbara Stanwyck in *Double Indemnity,* Marlene Dietrich in *The Blue Angel,* and Mae Murray in the silent film *Circe.*

filet mignon (1906), from French "dainty fillet," is the name given to the small, thick round of steak cut from the narrow end of a beef tenderloin.

filigree (1693), from French **filigrane,** "watermark" (from Italian **filigrana,** "thread of grains"), is a term applied to delicate ornamental work of silver, gold, or copper wires, especially to the lacy, intricate metalwork of jewelers. The word is also used of patterns or designs resembling such fine openwork, as in **a filigree of frost** on the windowpane.

flamboyant (1832), from French **flamboyant** "flaming, flashing," the present participle of the verb **flamboyer,** "to blaze, to flare, to flash," is an adjective meaning "strikingly bold or brilliant, dashing, given to colorful or florid behavior." George Eliot, in her 1876 novel *Daniel Deronda,* described one of her characters as being "with massive face, flamboyant hair."

foyer (1859), the lobby of a theater or hotel, the vestibule or entry hall of a house or apartment, comes from French **foyer,** "fireplace, hearth" (from Latin **focus,** "hearth"). The foyer was originally a room to which theater audiences went to warm themselves between the acts of a play.

fracas (1727), a disorderly brawl, a noisy quarrel, comes from French **fracas,** "din, row" (from Italian **fracasso,** which is related to the verb **fracassare,** "to shatter, to smash, to break up completely").

franglais (1964), a corrupt version of the French language marked by a large number of borrowed English words and phrases, comes from mixing **francais,** "French" with **anglais,** "English."

gaffe (1909), a social blunder or faux pas, comes from French "blunder," which is a special use of the word **gaffe,** signifying a boat hook used for landing large fish.

galosh (c. 1350), from Middle French **galoche** (from Medieval Latin **galopedium,** "a wooden shoe"), is now a waterproof overshoe, usually made of rubber, worn especially in snow and slush. In the fourteenth century, galoshes were wooden shoes or sandals fastened to the feet with leather thongs or clogs with heavy wooden soles and an upper part of leather or some other soft material. They were often used outdoors to protect the delicate shoes made of silk or other fabric that were worn underneath. The wooden galosh is found both in Langland's *Piers Plowman* and in Chaucer's *Canterbury Tales* ("The Squire's Tale": "Ne were worthy to unbokel his galoche"). By the seventeenth century, the word had acquired its current meaning, as in this November 15, 1665, entry from Samuel Pepys's diary: "My Lady Batten walking through the dirty lane with her new spick and span white shoes, she dropped one of her galoshes in the dirt."

gauche (1751), from French "left" or "left hand," is an adjective meaning "awkward, clumsy, lacking tact, sensitivity, or social grace." The noun **gaucherie** (1798) denotes the lack of social grace. The great British statesman Benjamin Disraeli, in his

1826 satirical novel *Vivian Grey*, described one of his characters as "an elegant lively lad, with just enough of dandyism to preserve him from committing gaucheries."

gazette (1605), a newspaper, is borrowed from French **gazette,** derived, in turn, from Italian (originally Venetian **gazeta**) **gazzetta,** which was a copper coin of small value, no doubt the price of a newspaper. Venetian **gazeta** was a diminutive of the word **gaza,** "magpie."

gigolo (1922), a man supported financially by a woman, generally a younger man living off an older woman in return for sexual favors and companionship, comes from French **gigolo,** the masculine equivalent of **gigolette,** a name given to prostitutes or to women who frequented public dance halls. Both French words were ultimately derived from Middle French **giguer,** "to frolic."

gouache (1882), a method of painting with opaque watercolors mixed with gum (and honey) so as to form a sort of paste, comes from French **gouache** (from Italian **guazzo,** "puddle, place where there is water," itself from Latin **aquatio,** "watering place"). The word is also used of the picture painted by gouache and of the pigment used in gouache. Among the outstanding artists who have used the gouache method are Georges Rouault, José Clemente Orozco, and Graham Sutherland.

harass (1618), to disturb or attack repeatedly, to vex persistently, to harry, to bother continually, comes from Middle French **harasser,** "to tire out," which started out as part of the phrase **courre à la harace,** "to pursue," formed from **harer,** "to incite dogs," since **hare** was an interjection used by French hunters to urge their dogs on.

i **mpasse** (1851), from French "no passing, dead end," is a predicament from which there is no escape, a deadlock, a stalemate, or a cul-de-sac, a dead end, an impassable road.

i **mpromptu** (1669), from French **impromptu,** "extemporaneous" (from Latin **in promptu** "in readiness, at hand"), as a noun, denotes a speech or performance given without premeditation or preparation, or a musical composition, especially for the piano, suggesting improvisation. As an adjective, **impromptu** means "done on the spur of the moment" or "suddenly or hastily improvised."

i **nfantry** (1579), a body of foot soldiers, military units trained to fight on foot with rifles, grenades, and other weapons, comes from French **infanterie** (from Italian **infanteria,** "group of youths, foot soldiers," ultimately from Latin **infans,** "small child, literally, one unable to speak").

i **ntrigue** (1612), to arouse the curiosity or interest of someone or to engage in secret schemes and plots, is borrowed from the French verb **intriguer,** "to rouse the interest, to plot, to scheme" (from Italian **intrigare,** itself from Latin **intricare,** "to entangle, to entrap"). The word **intrigue** is related etymologically to the word **intricate.** It is frequently used in the seventeenth century, by such writers as Samuel Pepys and John Dryden, to mean "to carry on an illicit love affair."

j **alousie** (1591), from French **jalousie,** "jealousy" (from Italian **gelosia,** "jealousy"), is the name given to a blind or shutter with adjustable horizontal slats used both to admit light and air and to exclude rain and the rays of the sun. **Jalousie** gets its name because blinds of this type would enable a viewer to spy (on his or her beloved's indiscretions) while remaining out of sight.

jaundice (1303), from Old French "yellowness," is the name given to a yellowish discoloration of the skin, eyes, tissues, and body fluids caused by an increase of bile pigments in the blood. Such a condition is often symptomatic of diseases such as hepatitis and sickle-cell anemia. The word is also used of a hostile attitude or feeling marked by views that are prejudiced or distorted because of envy or resentment.

jaunty (1662), easy and sprightly in manner or appearance, smart and stylish, is an Anglicized phonetic representation of the French word **gentil,** "noble, gentle"; that is, it was an attempt to reproduce the French word as it sounded to English ears. The word **jaunty** is related to the words **gentle, genteel,** and **gentile.**

latrine (1642), from French **latrine** (from Latin **latrina,** which is short for **lavatrina,** "place for washing"), is a toilet, privy, or receptacle (such as a pit or trench in the earth) used as a toilet in a camp or military barracks.

layette (1839), a complete outfit of clothing, toilet articles, and bedding for a newborn infant, comes from French **layette** (from Middle French **laiete,** "small coffer").

liaison (1809), from French "connection, bond," is the communication between units of the armed forces to ensure connected action, cooperation, and mutual understanding. The word is also used of the officer who is concerned with such cooperation and understanding. Since the 1820s, liaisons have also signified illicit sexual relationships. Actually, the word **liaison** appears in English as early as 1648 in the now obsolete sense of "a thickening for sauces which consists primarily of egg yolks."

lieutenant (c. 1375), a noun use of the Middle French phrase **lieu tenant,** "place holding," is the name given to a commissioned officer in the United States Navy ranking between lieutenant junior grade and lieutenant commander. In the police or fire department, a lieutenant is an officer who ranks below a captain. **Lieutenant** also signifies a person who acts as a representative of a higher official.

lingerie (1835), from French **lingerie** (from **linge,** "linen"), denotes sleepwear and various other items of intimate apparel worn by women, which are no longer necessarily made of linen.

love (1742), a tennis and whist term denoting a score of zero, may come from the French **l'oeuf,** "the egg," because of the resemblance of a zero to an egg. The etymology of the term **love** is uncertain and has been for more than two hundred years, as this quotation from a 1780 issue of *Gentleman's Magazine* will attest: "We are not told how, or by what means Six love comes to mean Six to nothing."

malaise (1768), from French "discomfort, ill ease," is a condition of bodily uneasiness or discomfort, often signaling the onset of a disease. The word also refers to a vague feeling of lethargy, lassitude, or mental ill-being.

mange (c. 1400), from Middle French **mangeue,** "an eating, an itch" (from the Middle French verb **mangier,** "to eat"), is the name given by veterinarians and dermatologists to any of various contagious skin diseases caused by parasitic mites and characterized by loss of hair, affecting domestic animals, such as sheep, dogs, horses, and pigs, as well as humans.

maraud (1711), to roam or go around in search of plunder, is borrowed from French **marauder,** "to plunder," formed from **maraud,** "a rogue, rascal, vagabond," which is probably related to French dialectal **maraud,** meaning "tomcat."

marquee (1690), a permanent rooflike shelter or canopy (made of metal or glass) projecting above a theater entrance and giving the name of a currently featured play or film and its stars, comes from French **marquée,** a modification of **marquise,** "marchioness" or "awning (on a pleasure boat)," perhaps from **marquer,** "to mark." In the seventeenth, eighteenth, and nineteenth centuries, **marquee** was used in English to signify an officer's field tent or one used at a public exhibition or fair.

mascot (1881), an animal, person, or object adopted by a group as its representative symbol, especially to bring good luck, comes from French **mascotte** (from Provençal **mascoto,** "talisman, charm," related to **masco,** "sorceress, witch"). The word became popular, even in English-speaking countries, shortly after the opera *La Mascotte* by Edmond Audran (1840–1901) opened in Paris at the Bouffes-Parisiens in December 1880. It is common practice in the United States for military academy and college football teams to adopt a mascot as, for example, U.S. Army (mule), U.S. Navy (goat), U.S. Air Force (falcon), Yale (bulldog), Princeton (tiger), Columbia (lion), Michigan (wolverine), Minnesota (gopher), Wisconsin (badger), Fordham (ram), Washington State (cougar), Oregon State (beaver), and Oregon (duck). Mascots are frequently brought to the game. The first Navy goat, El Cid, made his debut at the fourth annual Army-Navy game, in 1893.

massage (1876), the therapeutic art of manipulating the bodily tissues by rubbing, kneading, stroking, or tapping in order to relieve tension, stimulate circulation, and increase suppleness, comes from French **massage,** "rubbing down, massage," which, in turn, comes from the verb **masser,** "to rub down (the body)." The origin of **masser** is problematic. The word comes either from Arabic **massa,** "to handle," or from Portuguese **massa,** "dough." Massage therapy was one of the earliest forms of treatment used to alleviate symptoms due to disease or injury. Ancient Chinese and Hindu writings include massages in their list of medical procedures, and the Greek physician Hippocrates (c. 460–c. 377 B.C.) also alludes to the medical benefits of massage therapy. A **masseur** (1876) is a man, and a **masseuse** (1876) is a woman who practices massage as a profession.

matinee (1848), from French **matinée,** "morning," is a dramatic or musical performance held, not in the morning, as its etymology would suggest, but in the daytime, usually in the afternoon. During the first decade of the twentieth century, the phrase **matinee idol,** indicating a handsome actor especially attractive to matinee audiences, began to be used.

mayday or **May Day** or **may day** (1927), the international radio-telephone signal word used by ships and aircraft as a distress call, is borrowed from French **(venez) m'aider,** "(come) help me!"

medal (1586), a flat piece of metal, usually in the shape of a circle, cross, or star, often with an inscription or design, given as a reward for excellence or bravery or issued to commemorate a person or event, is borrowed from French **médaille** (from Italian **medaglia,** "copper coin worth half a denarius"). Ironically, then, a coin of minute value is now presented to acknowledge achievement of the highest value. Among the earliest academic medals recorded are gold medals awarded for the study of Greek, mentioned by George Berkeley in 1751. In English, **medallion** (1658), from French **médaillon,** "large medal" (from Italian **medaglione,** "large medal"), denotes, appropriately enough, a large medal. It is also applied to a permit issued by a governmental agency to cab drivers to operate their taxicabs and to a small round or oval serving of meat.

melee (1648), from French **mêlée**, "conflict, fray" (also from **mêler**, "to mix, to mingle, to throw into confusion"), is a confused, hand-to-hand skirmish among several people.

memoir (1567), often used in the plural, a record or account of one's personal life or of historical events written by a person who has firsthand knowledge of those events, is borrowed from French **mémoire**, "memory."

menu (1837), from French **menu**, "detailed list," a noun use of the adjective **menu**, "small, detailed" (from Latin **minutus**, "small"), is a list of the dishes served at a banquet, restaurant, or diner. Recently, **menu** has become a computer term, signifying a list of options shown on the display of the computer from which a user can choose an operation. In the seventeenth century, the word **menu,** short for French **menu peuple,** "little people," was used in English to refer to the common people or the mob, a use now obsolete.

meringue (1706), a frothy mix of stiffly beaten egg whites and sugar browned and used as a topping for pies and pastries and a small shell made of meringue and filled with fruit or ice cream, is borrowed from French **meringue,** which is perhaps related to the Walloon dialect **maringue,** "shepherd's loaf," a light afternoon meal. Attempts to link meringues with the town of Meiringen in the Bern canton of Switzerland are unconvincing.

mirage (1803) is an optical illusion, especially at sea or in a desert, by which the image of an object appears above, below, or to one side of its true position or a pool of water appears at some distance from the spectator, where no water actually exists. Mirages are caused by the bending of rays of light by a layer of heated air of varying density. **Mirage** is borrowed from French **mirage,** which is formed from the verb **mirer,** "to look at." The most spectacular type of mirage is the fata morgana, which consists of breathtaking illusions, such as mountain ranges or castles in the air, where the images bear little or no resemblance to the actual objects that have given rise to them.

mitten (1386) a covering for the hand with no division for the four fingers but having a separate section for the thumb, is borrowed from Middle French **mitaine.** The word first appears in English in Chaucer's *Canterbury Tales* (the "Prologue to the Pardoner's Tale").

morgue (1821), a place in which dead bodies, often the bodies of victims of violent crimes or accidents, are kept until identified and claimed by relatives or released for burial, is borrowed from French **morgue,** the name of the building in Paris housing unidentified dead bodies. **Morgue** is also used of the reference collection of a newspaper office consisting of clippings, books, and other materials, often assembled for the future obituaries of persons still living.

motif (1848), a recurrent theme, character, idea, or subject, especially in a literary or musical work, or a recurrent form or shape in a design (in a painting or on wallpaper), comes from French **motif,** "motive" (from Latin **motivus,** "serving to move"), since the motif serves to move forward and develop the work of art in which it appears.

musketeer (1590), from French **mousquetaire,** "one who uses a musket," is a soldier armed with a musket—a heavy, large-caliber smoothbore gun carried by infantry. Undoubtedly, the most rousing account of the daily lives and activities of musketeers can be found in Alexandre Dumas *père*'s 1844 novel *The Three Musketeers,* a breathlessly exciting and immensely charming historical novel set in the time of King Louis XIII and his minister, Cardinal Richelieu.

mustache (1585), the hair growing on the upper lip, usually of men, comes from Middle French **moustache** (from Old Italian **mostaccio**).

mutton (c. 1290), the flesh of mature sheep used as food, comes from Old French **moton,** "ram."

naive (1654), from French **naïve,** the feminine of **naïf** "natural, instinctive" (ultimately from Latin **nativus,** "native"), is an adjective meaning "without experience or worldly wisdom, unsophisticated, ingenuous, simple, artless, credulous." The noun **naiveté** was first recorded in English in 1673.

negligee (1756), a long, flowing dressing gown or robe, often made of a sheer material, worn by women, is borrowed from French **negligée,** "unheeded, neglected, slovenly," the feminine past participle of the verb **negliger,** "to neglect, to slight." It is somewhat incongruous that the negligee, which suggests careless, unkempt, and incomplete attire, has today become one of the more expensive and fashionable items in a woman's wardrobe.

nonchalance (1678), an air of casualness, cool indifference, or lack of concern, and **nonchalant** (1734), an adjective meaning "cool, calm, and collected," are both derived from the obsolete French verb **nonchaloir**, "to lack warmth, to disregard, to be indifferent."

nougat (1827), from French **nougat** (from Latin **nux**, "nut"), is a chewy confection of almonds or other kinds of nuts and sometimes fruit pieces in a sugar paste.

nuance (1781), from French **nuance**, "shade, hue," which is ultimately derived from the Latin **nubes**, "cloud," signifies both a delicate difference or variation in shade or tone and a subtle distinction in expression, opinion, or meaning.

nuisance (c. 1410), an annoying, unpleasant, or obnoxious person, thing, or condition, comes from Old French **nuiser**, "to harm." Originally, the meaning was more abstract, denoting injury, harm, or annoyance.

oboe (1724), a woodwind instrument with a conical tube and a double-reed mouthpiece, comes, via Italian, from French **hautbois** "high wood" (**haut**, "high," plus **bois**, "wood"). The oboe descended from an instrument called a shawm and was already in use in the seventeenth century, although it was not really developed until the eighteenth century and not completely perfected until the nineteenth.

omelette, also spelled **omelet** (1611), eggs beaten until frothy, sometimes combined with other ingredients (parsley, chives, chopped ham, fish, cheese, mushrooms, apples, or jelly, for example), and cooked without stirring until set, comes from French **omelette**, a variation of Middle French **alemelle**, "thin plate, the blade of a sword or knife." The omelette was named from its thin, flat shape and was first described in English (in 1611) as a "pancake of eggs."

palette (1622), from Middle French **palette,** "spade, little shovel," is a thin oval or rectangular board with a thumb hole at one end, used by a painter for holding and mixing colors.

panache (1553), flair, verve, style, flamboyance in style and action, comes from Middle French **pennache** (from Old Italian **pennachio,** "little wing, little feather"). The word was first used in English to denote an ornamental tuft or plume of feathers on a helmet—a meaning it still carries.

parfait (1894), a cold dessert made of alternating layers of ice cream and fruit (or syrup), normally topped with whipped cream and served in a tall, slender, short-stemmed glass, comes from the French word for "perfect." The word is also applied to a flavored egg custard containing whipped cream and syrup that has been frozen without stirring.

parole (1616), from Middle French **parole,** which was short for **parole d'honneur,** "word of honor," was originally a promise given by a prisoner of war that he or she would return to custody on a specified day or would refrain from taking up arms against his or her captors for a stated period. Today, **parole** usually refers to the release of a person from prison before the entire sentence has been served.

patois (1643), from French **patois,** "clumsy speech" (from Old French **patoier,** "to handle clumsily"), is a linguistic term designating a dialect or regional form of a language that differs from the standard or literary form of the language. More specifically, it often refers to the Creole speech of the English-speaking Caribbean. Sometimes, too, it is synonymous with "cant" or "jargon."

pedigree (c. 1412), an ancestral line or a genealogical chart or record, especially of purebred animals, such as horses, dogs, and cats, is borrowed from Middle French **pie(d) de grue,** "foot of crane," since the shape made by the three-lined marks of a genealogical chart supposedly bears a resemblance to a crane's foot. In the seventeenth century, pedigrees were kept of bees.

petit four (1884), a small cake, sometimes cut from pound or sponge cake and frosted and decorated, is borrowed from French **petit four,** "small oven." The name **petit four** is given to a wide variety of small cakes, including macaroons, tuiles, wafers, and especially Genoise cut into tiny squares and coated with an apricot glaze and covered with fondant frosting.

petty (1393), from French **petit,** "small," is an adjective in English meaning "of little or no importance," "exhibiting narrow ideas or interests," "ungenerous and small-minded."

picayune (1804), from French **picaillon,** "halfpenny" (from Provençal **picaio,** "money"), means "trivial" or "petty." It was originally the name of a coin used in Louisiana and Florida that was equal to half a Spanish real.

picnic (1748), from French **pique-nique** (or possibly from German **Picknick**), is an excursion or outing with food usually provided by the participants and eaten in the open air. The word first appears in English in reference to foreign countries, Germany and France in particular, as, for example, when Lord Chesterfield wrote to his son in Germany (in 1748): "I like the description of your Pic-nic." It is not mentioned before 1800 as an English custom. At the beginning of the nineteenth century, however, the Picnic Society was formed in London by a group of fashionable people to sponsor social entertainments and private theatricals, to which each member contributed a share. An article in the 1802 *London Times* described the rules of the club: "The subscribers to the entertainment have a bill of fare presented to them, with a number against each dish. The lot which he draws obliges him to furnish the dish marked against it, which he either takes with him in his carriage, or sends by a servant." The members of the new society were called, unsurprisingly, Picnickians.

piquant (1630), pleasantly pungent, agreeably sharp or biting in taste, engagingly provocative, stimulating, or attractive, comes from French **piquant,** "pricking," formed from the verb **piquer,** "to prick, to sting, to quilt." The English verb **pique** (1532), to anger, to arouse resentment, to wound (the pride of), to excite (curiosity or interest), to provoke to action, is borrowed from Middle French **pique** (which, like **piquant,** comes from the verb **piquer**). The English word, **piqué** (1837), which is the name given to a durable fabric of cotton, rayon, or silk with raised cords, to a ballet step in which the dancer steps onto the tip of the toe without bending the knees, and to decoration with punched or stippled patterns, also comes from the French verb **piquer. Piquet** (1646), a two-handed card game with a pack of thirty-two cards (the cards from deuces to sixes being eliminated), may also be borrowed from the French verb **piquer,** "to prick." Some linguists have argued, on the other hand, that the name of the game is derived from **pic,** a term that is used in the game, or from **pique,** "a spade (in a deck of cards)."

piston (1704), from French **piston** (from Italian **pistone,** a variation of **pestone,** "a large pestle," formed from **pistare,** "to beat, to pound"), is a sliding piece moved by or moving against fluid pressure. It ordinarily consists of a disk or cylindrical part tightly fitting within a cylinder along which it moves back and forth.

pivot (1611), from French **pivot,** "pivot, hinge, axis, swivel, fulcrum (of a lever)," is a short shaft or pin, usually made of metal and pointed, on the end of which something rests and turns or about which something rotates. It also signifies anyone or anything on which anyone or anything else turns, as, for example, a person (or event) playing a central role or exerting a major influence. Pivoting in basketball consists of keeping one foot in place while holding the ball and moving the other foot one step in any direction to avoid being charged with walking.

plateau (1796), from French **plateau,** "tray, platter, flat object," is no longer used, as it was by George Washington and his contemporaries, to indicate an ornamental tray or dish for table service. Today, the closest that a plateau comes to a table is the synonym **tableland.** A plateau is an extensive tract of land having a relatively flat surface that is elevated above the adjoining land. Today, a plateau denotes, too, a relatively stable period or condition in which there is little growth or decline.

plumage (1481), the entire covering of feathers on a bird, comes from Middle French **plumage** (related to **plume,** "feather"). The English word **plume,** which denotes a feather, often large and fluffy and worn as a hat ornament, also comes from French **plume.** Since the 1940s, **plume** has been used regularly to describe an elongated and mobile column of smoke rising from factories and the chimneys in homes.

pompon or **pompom** (1861), from French **pompon,** apparently a repetitive formation based on the word **pompe,** "pomp, ceremony, display," is an ornamental tuft or ball of wool used on hats and slippers, a flower-shaped cluster of streamers waved by cheerleaders, or a chrysanthemum or dahlia with a globe-shaped flower. The word appears in English as early as 1748, but it was spelled **pong-pong.**

porcupine (1423), one of several relatively large rodents having stiff, sharp, barbed spines or quills, comes from Middle French **porc d'espine,** "thorny pig." As many fallacies are attached to porcupine lore as are quills to their bodies. For example, contrary to popular belief, the porcupine does not eject its quills, even though some are occasionally detached when it shakes itself. The North American porcupine presents its rear to an approaching enemy. Once attacked, it thrusts its tail against its adversary so that the quills detach from its body and become embedded in the assailant. **Porpentine** was the form of the word known to Shakespeare, who used it seven times in his works, as, for example, when the Duke of York compares John Mortimer to a "sharp-quill'd porpentine" in *Henry VI, Part Two,* and when the ghost of Hamlet's father tells Hamlet that he "could a tale unfold" that would make "each particular hair" on Hamlet's head "stand on end, Like quills upon the fretful porpentine."

porpoise (1309), a small, largely black mammal of the whale family with a blunt, rounded snout, or any of several dolphins (like the bottle-nosed dolphin), comes from Middle French **porpois,** "pig fish, hog fish" (from Medieval Latin **porcopiscis**). The first-century Roman author Pliny the Elder called the cetacean a **porcus marinus,** "sea pig."

portcullis (c. 1330), from Middle French **porte coleice,** "sliding door," is a heavy frame or grating of iron, especially in a medieval castle, that is hung over the gateway of a fortified place and lowered between vertical grooves as a defense against assault.

portrait (1570), the likeness or representation of a person, especially of the face, in a painting, drawing, or photograph, or a literary description of a person, is borrowed from Middle French **portrait** (past participle of the verb **portraire**, "to depict, to draw forth").

prairie (1682), from French **prairie**, "meadow," is a tract of level or slightly undulating grassy land, generally without trees. The prairies in the Mississippi valley have deep, highly fertile soil; tall, coarse grasses; and few trees.

precipice (1598), from Middle French **precipice** (from Latin **praecipitium**, "a falling headlong, a steep place"), originally denoted a headlong fall or descent in English. Today it signifies either a cliff with a vertical or very steep face of rock or a dangerous situation.

premiere (1889), the first public performance or showing of an opera, play, or film, a "first night," comes from French **première**, which is short for **première representation**, "first performance."

procedure (1611), from French **procedure** (from Latin **procedere**, "to go forward"), is a particular way of proceeding or acting in a situation or process, especially an established or customary way of doing things.

purée (1707), borrowed from French **purée**, "strained, mashed" (formed from the verb **purer**, "to strain, to purify"), is a cooked food, often a vegetable or fruit, that has been passed through a sieve or a blender. It also refers to a kind of broth or soup made from vegetables, meat, or fish that has been boiled and put though a blender.

ramp (1778), an inclined plane connecting two levels, a movable stairway for entering or leaving the cabin door of an airplane, comes from French **rampe**, "slope, incline (of hill), pitch (of roof), rise" (from Old French **ramper**, "to creep, to crawl, to climb").

rappel (1931), from French **rappel**, "backward motion, recall," is a mountaineering term that refers to a method of descending a cliff by means of a rope placed under the left thigh and over the right shoulder; the rope is gradually played out.

regime (1776), from French "rule, government," indicates a manner or form of government, a system that has widespread influence, a government in power, or a period of rule.

republic (1604), a government in which the supreme power resides in the body of people entitled to vote and is exercised by representatives responsible to them, a state whose head is not a king or similar ruler, comes from French **république** (from Latin **res publica**, "the public entity").

reservoir (1690), from French **réservoir**, "storage place, tank" (related to the Middle French verb **reserver**, "to retain, keep back"), is a place, natural or artificial, usually made of earthwork or masonry, where water is collected and kept in quantity for ordinary use. Reservoirs and dams have been in use for more than four thousand years. The oldest dam in the world is the Sadd el-Kafara Dam in Egypt, built about 2700 B.C., whose ruins are still visible. In China, Emperor Yau built dams and reservoirs to provide water for his people around 2280 B.C. In Libya, the ancient Romans built complex systems of low masonry reservoirs to supply water for towns, the most famous of which was located in Leptis Magna.

restaurant (1827), a public eating place, is borrowed from **restaurant,** a noun use of the present participle of the French verb **restaurer,** "to restore, to refresh." The use of French **restaurant** in the sense of a restorative place where refreshments are served to customers originated in Paris in 1765. The first appearance of the word in English occurs in James Fenimore Cooper's 1827 novel *The Prairie:* "At the most renowned of the Parisian restaurans . . ."

revenue (c. 1430), from Middle French **revenue** "(something) returned," a noun use of the past participle of **revenir,** "to return, to come back," is the term applied to the income that a government collects from taxation, customs, and other sources and sets aside for the payment of public expenses. Except for one use in English of **revenue** to mean "a return to a place" (dating back to 1422), the word has also signified (since 1433) the return or yield from any kind of property or service. Shakespeare, in Sonnet 142, complains that his lover's lips have "profan'd their scarlet ornaments and . . . robb'd others' beds' revenues of their rents."

reverie (1657), a daydream or state of dreamy musing, is borrowed from French **rêverie,** "musing, idle fancy" (from Middle French "delirium," related to the verb **rêver,** "to wander, to speak wildly, to be delirious"). In music, a reverie is an instrumental composition of a dreamy nature. In the fourteenth century, Chaucer used the word **reverie** as a synonym for wantonness in *The Canterbury Tales* ("The Reeve's Tale") and to denote a state of joy or delight in his *Romance of the Rose*. **Reverie** is related etymologically to the English word **rave.**

revue (1872), a theatrical entertainment featuring satirical skits, songs, and dances, often parodying current events, the latest fads, and newsworthy celebrities, comes from French "review," a noun use of the past participle of the verb **revoir,** "to see again." The revue originated in France in the early nineteenth century and was introduced into England by James Robertson Planche in 1825 with his *Success; or a Hit if You Like It.* The revue began to enjoy great popularity in Great Britain and the United States in the 1890s. *Under the Clock*, a revue satirizing current theater rather than current events, opened in England in 1893, and *The Passing Show*, closer to vaudeville than revue, was produced the next year in the United States by Charles Lederer. In the twentieth century, such revues as Ziegfeld's *Follies*, George White's *Scandals*, *The Garrick Gaieties*, and *Cocoanuts* (starring the Marx Brothers) marked the heyday of the revue. The revue declined in the 1930s and (with the exception of an occasional hit show like *Pins and Needles* or *Beyond the Fringe*) has almost completely disappeared from the stage. Television has attempted to revive the form in such satirical shows as *That Was the Week That Was*, which ran in the 1960s, and the long-running *Saturday Night Live*.

rice (1234), from Old French **ris** (from Greek **oryza**), is the name given to the starchy seeds of an annual cereal grass cultivated in warm climates and used for food. The earliest record of rice production dates from about 2800 B.C. in China, and the word appears in Indian records as early as 2000 B.C. Alexander the Great and the Greeks were first introduced to the crop when they invaded India in the fourth century B.C. When the Moors conquered Spain in 700 A.D., they brought rice with them. The Spanish carried it to Italy in 1400 and to South America and the West Indies two hundred years later. There is a story that a certain Captain J. Thurber was sailing from Madagascar in 1685, his brigantine laden with rice, when a storm blew his ship off course to South Carolina. Rescued by colonists in Charleston, Thurber showed his gratitude by giving them a small amount of seed rice, from which South Carolina eventually developed into the leading rice-producing state in the United States.

ricochet (1769), the motion of an object as it glances or skips along a surface with a series of rebounds, is borrowed from French **ricochet,** "the skipping of a stone on the water."

rococo (1836), from French **rococo,** a fanciful formation based on **rocaille,** "pebble work, rock work," is the name given to a style of architecture, landscape gardening, porcelain, and furniture decoration that originated in France during the reign of Louis XV in the eighteenth century. Rococo is marked by its ornamentation, often considered excessively or tastelessly florid, of scrollwork, shellwork, vines, and flowers. Rococo paintings, as, for example, those of the French artists François Boucher and Jean-Honoré Fragonard, are characterized by delicacy of color, small details, and the choice of exuberantly frivolous subject matter. Rococo music is noted for its superficial refinement and charm, its lack of passion, and its use of elaborate ornamentation.

rouge (1753), any of a variety of red powders used to lend an artificial redness to the cheeks or lips, is borrowed from French **rouge,** "red." The word also indicates a reddish powder (formerly called **jewelers' red rouge**) consisting largely of ferric oxide and used for polishing metal and glass.

roulette (1745), from French **roulette,** "little wheel," is a game of chance played in gambling casinos throughout the world at a table marked off with numbers from one to thirty-six, one or two zeros, and other sections offering various betting opportunities. In the center is set a wheel (which gives roulette its name), into which a small ivory or plastic ball is spun. When the ball slows and comes to rest in one of the thirty-seven (or thirty-eight) compartments, the winning number is indicated, together with characteristics important to the game (whether the number is, for example, odd or even, red or black, between one and eighteen or between nineteen and thirty-six). In European casinos, the roulette wheel has only one compartment marked zero, thereby reducing the house advantage over the player. Since the nineteenth century, the word **roulette** has also indicated a small wheel with sharp teeth used by engravers and other craftsmen for making lines of marks, dots, or perforations.

routine (1676), a regular course or procedure, everyday chores, tasks and activities performed regularly or at specified intervals, is borrowed from French **routine**, "little course, little way," the diminutive of **route**, "way, course," from Latin **rupta (via)**, "broken (road)".

sabotage (1891), the malicious destruction of an employer's property by workmen, usually during a strike, the obstruction of an industrial process by enemy agents (during wartime) or by workers (during a trade dispute) to slow it down or bring it to a halt, or any undermining of a cause, comes from French **sabotage**, "foul play," formed from the verb **saboter**, "to botch, to execute badly, to wreck willfully, to clatter one's wooden shoes **(sabots)**." In many ways, it seems appropriate that the word **sabotage** be borrowed from French, since the clandestine activities of the French underground, or Maquis, during the German occupation of France in World War II, go unrivaled in sheer destructiveness. By dynamiting trains, bridges, and roads, destroying machinery in factories, kidnapping or murdering key personnel, the French saboteurs undermined completely the German cause.

salad (c. 1390), a usually cold dish of herbs or green vegetables, such as lettuce, endive, and spinach, as well as tomatoes, radishes, and cucumbers, served with a dressing, or a dish of meat, seafood, eggs, pasta, or fruit, usually cut up, mixed, and served cold with a dressing, comes from Middle French **salade**, "salted" (ultimately from Latin **sal**, "salt"). In Shakespeare's *All's Well That Ends Well*, the clown says of Helena to Lafeu and the countess of Rousillon: "She was the sweet marjoram of the sallet, or rather the herb of grace." The word **salad** is etymologically related to the words **salary, saline, sausage, sauce,** and **salami,** all of which share the same Latin root, **sal,** "salt."

salmon (c. 1300), a large soft-finned marine and freshwater food fish with pink flesh, found along the northern Atlantic coasts of Europe and northern Pacific (whose rivers it enters to breed), is borrowed from Old French **saumon**, which comes from Latin **salmo, salmonis**, a derivative of the verb **salire**, "to leap."

S alon (1699), from French **salon,** "big hall," is a large drawing room or reception room in a fashionable home; an assemblage of notable literary figures, artists, or statesmen; or a hall used for the exhibition of works of art. In France, in the nineteenth century, the Salon was an annual exhibition of works or painting and sculpture by living artists. Originally held in the Salon d'Apollon of the Louvre, the Salon became increasingly controversial, since it tended to prefer works that were academic and safe to the innovative and daring (such as Manet's now famous *Déjeuner sur l'herbe,* which was rejected by the Salon). In 1863, the Salon des Refusés, an exhibition of rejected works, was set up by Napoleon III to display pictures rejected by the official Salon. Since 1913, the word **salon** has also been used in English to signify an establishment run by a hairdresser or beauty specialist.

S aloon (1728), a variation of the French **salon,** is, in the United States, a place for the sale and consumption of alcoholic drinks or a large cabin for the social use of the passengers on a ship. In the eighteenth century, **saloon** was synonymous with **salon.** The connection with alcoholic beverages began in the nineteenth century, when **saloon** was first used in England to denote a grog shop or the refreshment bar in a theater.

S auce (1350), a fluid dressing or soft, semiliquid topping eaten as a gravy or as a relish on some article of food, or stewed fruit, usually pureed, sweetened, and eaten with other food or as a dessert, comes from Middle French **sauce,** which was derived from late Latin **salsa,** "salted" (from **sal,** "salt").

S ausage (c. 1450), finely chopped pork, beef, or other meat mixed with various spiced and flavored seasonings and stuffed into casings of prepared animal intestines and made in links, comes from Old French **sausiche,** which was derived from late Latin **salsicia,** "seasoned with salt" (from **sal,** "salt").

Shanty (1820), a small crudely built hut, cabin, or house, comes from Canadian French **chantier,** "lumber camp, hut," a variation of French **chantier,** "dump, stand for barrels, yard, depot, gantry" (ultimately from Latin **cant(h)erius,** "rafter, prop, horse in poor condition, nag").

Souvenir (1775), borrowed from French **souvenir,** "keepsake, remembrance, memory," is a small article, generally not very expensive, that is purchased, given, or kept as a reminder of a place visited or a special event. **Souvenir** was first used in English (in 1775) as a synonym for **memory.**

Svelte (1817), from French **svelte,** "slender, slim" (from Italian **svelto,** "nimble, slender, elegant," which is formed from the verb **svellere,** "to pluck out, to root out"), is an adjective meaning variously "lithe," "slender," "willowy," "suave," "urbane," or "elegant."

tambourine (1579), a small drum, especially a shallow wooden hoop with a skin or parchment stretched over it and several pairs of small cymbals attached to the frame, played by shaking, striking with the hand, or rubbing with the thumb, comes from Middle French **tambourin,** "small drum" (ultimately from Arabic **tanbūr**).

terrain (1766), a piece or tract of land, especially when considered with reference to its physical features or tactical advantages, comes from French **terrain,** "ground, land, field, site" (ultimately from Latin **terra,** "land"). Today, **terrain** is a word used for both golf links and a croquet court.

terrier (1440), any of several breeds of usually small, intelligent dogs, used originally by hunters to pursue game, such as fox, otters, and badgers, and drive it out of its holes or hiding places, is borrowed from Middle French **(chien) terrier** "dog of the earth," from Medieval Latin **terrarius,** "pertaining to the earth." The terrier is so named because it was used to engage badgers underground or drive them out. Terrier breeds include the Airedale, Bedlington, bull, Cairn, Dandie Dinmont (named after a fictional farmer in Sir Walter Scott's 1814 novel *Guy Mannering*), fox, Kerry Blue, Lakeland, Scottish (called the Scottie), Sealyham, Skye, West Highland White terriers, and the miniature Schnauzer (which, unlike most terriers, was bred in Germany rather than the British Isles).

tête-à-tête (1697), a private conversation between two people, comes from French "head to head."

tic (1800), a sudden painless and habitual spasmodic motion of certain muscles, or a persistent trait, comes from French **tic,** which is onomatopoeic. It was originally the name of an equine disease—**ticq** or **ticquet**—a condition in which a horse's breath suddenly stops, causing the horse to stop and stand still.

timbre (1849), from French **timbre,** "bell, sound (of bell)," is the quality given to a sound by its overtones, be it the characteristic quality of tone produced by a particular musical instrument or voice, or the resonance by which the ear recognizes and identifies a voiced speech sound. In the fourteenth century, **timbre** was used in English to signify the crest over the shield in a coat of arms.

tirade (1801), a prolonged volley of bitter or angry words, a long vituperative or harsh speech, is borrowed from French **ti-rade,** "a stretch, a (continuous) pulling, a long speech," which, in turn, is from Italian **tirata,** "a volley, (something) drawn, pulled, or fired."

toilet (1540), from French **toilette**, "small cloth, doily, dressing table," a diminutive of the word **toile**, originally meant a wrapper for clothes. By the seventeenth century, the English word signified the act of dressing or grooming oneself, especially of arranging one's hair, as well as the table on which the items used for dressing oneself were placed. By the early nineteenth century, the word denoted a dressing room, especially one that contained a bath. But it has only been in the twentieth century that **toilet** has been applied to a bathroom, a lavatory, and to a bathroom fixture consisting of bowl, seat, lid, and flushing device used for urination and defecation.

toupee (1727), a wig or patch of false hair worn to cover up a bald spot, comes from French **toupet**, "tuft of hair, forelock." In the eighteenth century, the word **toupee** was used in English to signify a curl or artificial lock of hair made into a topknot on a periwig.

tourniquet (1695), from French **tourniquet**, "turnstile," which is formed from the verb **tourner**, "to turn," is the name of a device (as a bandage tightened by twisting a rigid bar put through it) that is used to check bleeding or blood flow by compressing a blood vessel. The word is also used of a device made of twisted cords that pulls the parts of a wooden piece of furniture together.

triage (1918), borrowed from French **triage**, "sorting," which is formed from **trier**, "to sort, to pick, to winnow," is the process of sorting casualties of battles and victims of disasters, to determine medical priority in the allocation of treatment in order to maximize the number of survivors. The word is now used in hospital emergency rooms by doctors and staff assigning degrees of urgency to wounds or illnesses. Because of the **tri-**, "three," root, it is commonly believed that patients are divided into three categories: those who will die even if they receive immediate treatment, those who will recover even if treatment is delayed, and those for whom immediate treatment would make a life-or-death difference. In France, the word was originally applied to the process of separating broken coffee beans from whole ones and to the chaff left by such winnowing.

trousseau (1817), the personal possessions of a bride, including her clothing and household linens, comes from French **trousseau,** "bunch (of keys), outfit, kit," which is formed from the verb **trousser,** "to tuck up, to pack up," which, in turn, comes from Middle French **troussel,** "little parcel, little bundle (of straw)."

tutu (1913), a short, full skirt, made of layers of stiff frills, worn by ballerinas, comes from French **tutu,** "ballet skirt," which is generally accepted to be a childish alteration of **cucu,** a diminutive of **cul,** "anus, rear end, bottom," which is the part of a ballerina's body most affected by the tutu.

unique (1602), from French **unique** (derived from Latin **unicus,** "only, sole, alone in its kind"), means "existing as the sole example," "unparalleled," "unusual," and "incomparable." There are those who object to the placement of words like **very, rather,** and **somewhat** before the adjective **unique** in English, arguing that **unique** has an absolute sense, but most English dictionaries simply do not support such an assumption.

vague (1548), from Middle French **vague** (derived from Latin **vagus,** "wandering"), is an adjective meaning "not clearly stated," "indefinite," "indistinct," "not sharply outlined," or "not definitely established or confirmed." The word **vague** is etymologically related to such English words as **vagrant, vagabond,** and **vagary.**

Valet (1567), a male servant who performs personal services for his master (such as taking care of his clothes), comes from French **valet** (Middle French **va(s)let**), "squire." The word **valet** is etymologically related to the English word **vassal,** a person in the Middle Ages who was granted the use of land in return for rendering homage and fealty (and often military service) to a feudal lord. The word is also linked to the English **varlet,** "a knave, rascal, rogue." Since 1960, the word **valet** has been used to signify an attendant who parks cars for patrons of restaurants and hotels.

Valise (1615), a traveling bag or small piece of luggage used to carry toilet articles and clothing, comes from French **valise** (from Italian **valigia**).

Velour or **velours** (1706), from French **velours,** "velvet," which comes, in turn, from Latin **villosus,** "hairy," is a fabric with a pile or napped surface that resembles velvet and is used for clothing, curtains, and upholstery. The word is also applied to a velvety fur felt used in the making of hats.

Vignette (1751), a brief evocative literary sketch of a person or place, an ornamental or decorative design, or a small illustration used on the title page of a book or at the beginning or end of a chapter, comes from French **vignette,** "little vine," since the decorations in early books were frequently vinelike in appearance.

Vogue (1571), from Middle French **vogue,** "rowing, course" (from Old Italian **voga,** formed from the verb **vogare,** "to row, to sail"), signifies a period of popularity, popular favor, or something that is fashionable at a particular time. It is similar to French **au courant,** "in the current," another water image used to suggest that one is fashionable or up-to-date.

Volunteer (1600), one who freely offers himself or herself for a service or undertaking or, more specifically, one who enters the military service of his own free will rather than through the draft, is borrowed from French **volontaire** (originally **voluntaire**), "self-willed, voluntary."

Zest (1709), signifying hearty enjoyment or gusto, liveliness or spirit, an agreeable flavor, or the peel or thin outer skin of a citrus fruit used as flavoring, is borrowed from **zest** (now **zeste**), the French word for orange or lemon peel. The oil squeezed from orange and lemon zest is also used to flavor liqueur, as a character from Lawrence Durrell's 1958 novel *Mountolive* remarks: "How good the taste of Dubonnet with a *zeste de citron*." The word **zeste,** interestingly enough, is sometimes used today in France to indicate the thick skin or woody partitions in a walnut.

German

angst (1849), a feeling of anxiety or insecurity, neurotic fear, remorse, comes from German **Angst,** "fear, anxiety." The German word originally meant "constriction," since it was formed from **eng,** "narrow," and **-st,** an abstract noun suffix. The English novelist George Eliot, author of *Middlemarch* and *Silas Marner*, used the word **Angst** in one of her letters (August 5, 1849): " 'Die Angst' she says often brings on a pain at her heart." Perhaps the best description in English of the meaning of **angst** is found in Palinurus's 1944 *Unquiet Grave*: "Angst may take the form of remorse about the past, guilt about the present, anxiety about the future."

delicatessen (1889), from German **Delikatessen,** the plural of **Delikatesse,** "delicacy" (from French **delicatesse**), is a store that sells ready-to-eat foods, such as cooked meats, cheese, and salads. The earliest reference to the word in English occurs in, of all places, an American newspaper, the *Kansas Times and Star* (November 7, 1889): "Burglars broke into Blake's delicatessen store . . . and . . . made an awful mess of the juicy stuff, canned and bottled."

dirndl (1937), a style of woman's dress with a close-fitting bodice, short sleeves, and full gathered skirt, in imitation of Tyrolean peasant wear, is borrowed from German **Dirndl,** which is short for **Dirndlkleid,** "young woman's dress" (from **Dirndl,** "young woman, girl," and **Kleid,** "dress").

dollar (1553), the name given to paper money or to a silver or cupronickel coin, equivalent to one hundred cents, comes from Low German or Dutch **daler** (from German **Taler,** short for **Joachimstaler,** a coin that was first minted in Joachimsthal in Bohemia in 1519, from a silver mine opened there in 1516). The dollar became the standard monetary unit of the United States in 1792, on the advice of Thomas Jefferson, who preferred a decimal system of coinage to the English system of pounds, shillings, and pence. Today, **dollar** (equal to one hundred cents) is the name given to the monetary units of Australia, the Bahamas, Barbados, Belize, Bermuda, Canada, Fiji, Guyana, Hong Kong, Jamaica, Liberia, New Zealand, Singapore, the Solomon Islands, Trinidad and Tobago, and Zimbabwe.

doppelganger (1851) or **double-ganger** (1830), an apparition, ghostly double, or counterpart of a living person, is borrowed from German **Doppelgänger,** "double-goer." The doppelganger plays an important role in such literary works as Edgar Allan Poe's "William Wilson," Hans Christian Andersen's "The Shadow," Fyodor Dostoevsky's *The Double*, and Joseph Conrad's *The Secret Sharer*. Variations of the doppelganger motif can be found in Robert Louis Stevenson's *Dr. Jekyll and Mr. Hyde*, Oscar Wilde's *The Picture of Dorian Gray*, and Nikolai Gogol's "The Nose," as well as in such films as Ingmar Bergman's *Persona*, Alfred

Hitchcock's *Psycho* and *Strangers on a Train*, Brian de Palma's *Dressed to Kill*, *Sisters*, *Obsession*, and *Body Double*, the Don Siegel, Philip Kaufman, and Abel Ferrara versions of *The Invasion of the Body Snatchers*, and Bryan Forbes's version of Ira Levin's *The Stepford Wives*.

gneiss (1757), borrowed from German **Gneiss** (from Middle High German **gneiste**, "spark"), is a metamorphic rock made up of bands rich in quartz and feldspar, alternating with bands containing micas.

hamster (1607), from German **Hamster** (derived from Old High German **hamastro** or Old Saxon **hamstra**, "corn-weevil"), is a short-tailed burrowing rodent with large cheek pouches, into which it stuffs food. The golden hamster has become an important laboratory animal and common household pet in the United States. The present captive population have probably all descended from a female and litter of twelve taken at Aleppo, Syria, in 1930.

haversack (1749), a single-strapped bag worn over one shoulder and used for carrying supplies or a soldier's bag for rations, comes, via French **havresac,** from German **Habersack** (from **Haber,** "oats," and **Sack,** "sack"). Originally, a haversack was the bag in which cavalry members carried oats for their horses. Later, the word was extended to a canvas bag used by travelers, especially French and English soldiers, to carry their personal belongings and their current day's rations.

hinterland or **hinterlands** (1890), back country, the remote or less developed parts of a country, the fringe areas of a town or city, or a region lying inland from a coast, comes from

German **Hinterland,** "behind-land." In his *Last Poems,* D. H. Lawrence used the word figuratively: "We are mostly unexplored hinterland."

hoodlum (1872), a thug, gangster, young ruffian or gang member, seems to come from a German dialect and is probably related to a derivative of the Swabian word for rag, **Hudel,** such as **hudelum,** "disorderly," **hudellam,** "weak, slack," or **Hudellump(e),** "rags, slovenly person." The word, which originated in San Francisco in the early 1870s, quickly spread to other parts of the United States by 1877. By this time, its etymology was already veiled in mystery. **Hoodlum** makes its earliest appearance in print in a February 1872 issue of the *Sacramento Weekly Union.*

kindergarten (1852), a school or class for children from four to six years old, is a German word that means "children's garden." Friedrich Froebel (1782–1852) is usually credited with the origin of the term **kindergarten.** Froebel was influenced by the writings of John Amos Comenius, who, in the early seventeenth century, stressed the importance of early childhood training, and those of Jean-Jacques Rousseau, who was no less convinced of the inherent goodness of children than he was of the nobility of savages. Unlike Robert Owen in England and Jean Denis Marie Cochin in France, who had set up educational institutions to care for the children of the poor, Froebel was committed to the early education of all children. Certain that children possessed within themselves dormant understanding of the universal truths, Froebel emphasized the importance of games and play, which he viewed as ritualistic keys to unlocking the secrets of life and nature. By 1872, thanks to the efforts of the Baroness Berta von Marenholtz-Bülow, kindergartens had spread throughout Europe. The first English-speaking kindergarten in the United States was introduced in Boston in 1860 by Elizabeth Palmer Peabody (1804–1894), who was, among other things, the sister-in-law of writer Nathaniel Hawthorne and educator Horace Mann. Thirteen years later, the first kindergarten in a public school was opened in St. Louis, Missouri, by Susan Elizabeth Blow, an educator so enamored of the teaching methods of the German educator that she founded, a year after her successful kindergarten venture, a training school for kindergarten teachers, and translated Froebel's *Mother Play*, a book of games and songs, into English. In 1887, the first kindergarten for the blind was established by the Perkins Institution and Massachusetts School for the Blind in Roxbury, Massachusetts. Not long afterward, in 1900, the first kindergarten for physically challenged children was opened at the Alta Settlement House in Cleveland, Ohio.

K **itsch** (1926), the term applied to art (or objets d'art) characterized by pretentiousness and a kind of tawdry insipidity, and created to appeal to popular or lowbrow taste, is borrowed from German **Kitsch,** "trash, refuse from the gutter," derived from the verb **kitschen,** "to throw together [a work of art]." Kitsch, often synonymous with the word **camp,** is often sentimental and always a success with the general public. Examples of kitsch range from Barbie dolls and Kewpie dolls to some of the more maudlin paintings of Norman Rockwell, the operettas of Sigmund Romberg, and the verse of Edgar Guest.

L **ager** (c. 1853), a light beer stored for aging, usually matured between six weeks to six months under refrigeration before use, comes from German **Lager,** short for **Lagerbier,** "storehouse (or lying) beer."

L **oafer** (1830), which is perhaps short for **landloafer** (from German **Landläufer,** "tramp, vagabond"), is a lazy person, one who spends his or her time in idleness. Since the late 1930s, the word has also been used of shoes designed to be worn on informal occasions. **Loafer** now is also a trademark for a slip-on shoe that resembles a moccasin.

m eld (1897), from German **melden,** "to announce, to inform, to notify," is the term used in a card game as, for example, pinochle, when one declares a card or combination of cards for a score, usually by placing them faceup on the table.

m uffin (1703), probably from Low German **Muffen,** "cakes," the plural of **Muffe,** "cake," is an individual cupshaped quick bread, often eaten toasted at breakfast or tea.

n oodle (1779), from German **Nudel,** is a ribbon-shaped strip of unleavened egg dough made with wheat, flour, and eggs, and served in soups and casseroles. The word **noodledom,** signifying foolishness or stupidity, was popular for a while in the early nineteenth century, as in "ninnies stock noodledom" (Robert Browning, "The Two Poets of Croisic") or "the noodledom of the magistrates is the one feature of the case. . . ." *The Star,* January 5, 1865).

p lunder (1632), which comes either from German **plundern,** "to sack, to despoil, to rob," or possibly from Dutch **plunderen,** "to rob of household goods," means "to rob (a place or person) of goods or valuables by force, as in war, theft, or fraud." The word was commonly used in Germany during the Thirty Years' War. The English, in alluding to the proceedings in Germany, borrowed the word. It became so familiar that by the time of the outbreak of their own civil war, in 1642, it was used to describe events in England. The Middle High German word **plunder** signified bedclothes and household goods. It was with this sense in mind that Meriwether Lewis, half of the famous Lewis and Clark Expedition in the United States, wrote this journal entry in 1805: "I dispatched Sergt. Ordway with 4 Canoes and 8 men to take up a load of baggage as far as Capt. Clark's camp and return for the remainder of our plunder."

poltergeist (1848), a mischievous ghost or spirit that makes its presence known by noises, knockings, and rappings, is borrowed from German **Poltergeist,** "noisy ghost," formed from **polter(n),** "to make noise, to knock, to rattle," and **Geist,** "ghost."

poodle (1820), a breed of curly-haired dog that has become the national dog of France, even though it probably originated in Germany as a water retriever, is borrowed from German **Pudel,** which is short for **Pudelhund,** "puddle dog," from **pudel(n),** "to splash," and **Hund,** "dog." The poodle, whose long frizzy or curly hair is often clipped and shaved in extravagant patterns, occurs in three sizes or varieties—standard, miniature, and toy. Drawings by the German artist Albrecht Dürer attest to the fact that the dog was popular in Germany in the fifteenth and sixteenth centuries. Paintings by Francisco Goya give evidence of the poodle's popularity as a pet in late-eighteenth-century Spain. In France, the poodle was commonly used as a traveling-circus trick dog.

pretzel (c. 1824), a crisp, dry biscuit baked in the form of a loose knot (or a stick) and flavored with salt, is borrowed from German **Pretzel,** a variation of **Bretzel,** which comes, ultimately, from Latin **bracellus,** "bracelet."

pumpernickel (1839), from German **Pumpernickel,** refers to a dark sourdough bread made from coarsely ground unbolted rye, which is associated especially with Westphalia. Many early tourists in Germany, like the English travel guide writer Thomas Nugent, in his 1756 *The Grand Tour,* found it "ill baked, and as black as coal." Most linguists agree that the word's meaning is every bit as coarse as the bread itself. **Pumpernickel** means "goblin's fart" and is derived from **pumpern,** "to break wind, to be flatulent," and **nickel,** "goblin," no doubt because of the reputed indigestibility of the bread. There is a farfetched (if ingenious) etymology of the word that involves Napoleon. The great French general, beating a hasty retreat from Moscow in 1812 on his favorite horse, Nichol, stopped to feed the horse some pumpernickel bread, which he called **pommes pour Nichol,** "apples for Nichol," which was how the bread supposedly got its name.

quartz (1756), from German **Quarz,** is a mineral consisting of silicon dioxide that occurs in hexagonal crystals or crystalline masses and varies in color or luster depending on the different impurities it contains.

rucksack (1866), a kind of knapsack worn by hikers, cyclists, and tourists, comes from German **Rucksack,** "back sack."

sauerkraut (1617), cabbage cut fine and fermented in brine until sour, comes from German **Sauerkraut,** "sour cabbage."

smut (1587), related to German **Schmutz,** "dirt, filth," which is derived from Middle High German **smutzen,** "to smear, to stain," signifies a black mark or smudge, a particle of soot, or a fungus disease of plants, especially cereal grasses, marked by the grains' being turned, wholly or partially, into dark powdery masses of spores. **Smut** is also used of indecent or obscene literature, language, and movies.

snorkel (1944), from German **Schnorchel,** "air intake," is a short rubber or plastic breathing tube used by swimmers, usually while moving just below the water's surface. The word was originally applied to an airshaft, invented in the Netherlands and developed in Germany, that permitted a diesel-engined submarine to remain submerged for long periods of time. The snorkel was designed to ventilate the submarine and allow the engines to discharge exhaust gases and foul air.

Spiel (1896), extravagant speech intended to persuade or lure people to buy or try something, a sales pitch, comes from German **Spiel,** "play, game," which was formed from the verb **spielen,** "to play, to gamble." It is also possible that the word was borrowed from the Yiddish word **shpil,** (related to the Yiddish verb **shpiln,** "to play, to gamble").

Swindler (1775), a confidence man, one who takes money or property from others by fraud or deceit, one who cheats or defrauds others, comes from German **Schwindler,** "giddy person, promoter of wild schemes, cheat," which is related to the verb **schwindeln,** "to be dizzy." A merchant with wild and extravagant schemes and predictions, especially in financial matters, was often the kind of person who would hoodwink the gullible and abscond with their money. The word is thought to have been introduced into London by German Jews toward the middle of the eighteenth century.

Vermouth (1806), an aperitif white wine flavored with wormwood or other aromatic herbs, roots, barks, and bitters, and often used in mixed drinks, as, for example, a martini, comes, via French **vermout(h),** from German **Wermuth** (now **Wermut**), "wormwood, absinthe."

Waltz (1781), a ballroom dance performed to music in triple time by couples who revolve in perpetual circles, taking one step to each beat, is borrowed from German **Walzer,** "a waltz," which was derived from the verb **walzen,** "to roll, to revolve, to dance." The waltz became fashionable in the early nineteenth century. The first composers to take the waltz seriously were Beethoven, Weber, and Schubert, while ballroom composers, such as the elder Johann Strauss and Joseph Lanner, his greatest rival, contributed to its enormous popularity in Vienna, whence the vogue quickly spread throughout Europe.

Wanderlust (1902), a strong desire or fondness for traveling about, comes from German **Wanderlust,** equivalent to wander(n), "to wander," and **Lust,** "desire."

Yodel (1827), from German **jodeln,** is to sing (or shout) by suddenly changing from one's ordinary voice to a falsetto and back again, in the manner of Swiss and Tyrolean mountaineers.

Zinc (1651), a bluish white metallic element brittle at ordinary temperatures but ductile between 200 and 250 degrees Fahrenheit, used as a protective covering for iron and steel, comes from German **Zink,** which was, in turn, probably derived from **Zinke(n),** "prong, tine," because of the spikelike form zinc takes in a furnace.

Zwieback (1894), a sweet egg-enriched biscuit or slice of raised bread baked and then toasted again in the oven until dry and crisp, is borrowed from German **Zwieback,** "twice-baked," equivalent to **zwie,** "twice," and **back(en),** "to bake."

Hebrew

behemoth (1382), an animal described in the fortieth chapter of the Book of Job, which may or may not be a hippopotamus, or any creature or thing of monstrous size or power, is borrowed from Hebrew **behemoth,** "great or monstrous beast," an augmentative plural of **behemah,** "beast." In Harriet Beecher Stowe's *Uncle Tom's Cabin,* the spoiled and endlessly complaining Marie St. Clare says ungraciously of her new slave Tom when her husband brings him in, "He's a perfect behemoth!"

cherub (c. 825), derived via Latin and Greek from Hebrew **kerubh** (pl. **kerūbhīm**), is a celestial being mentioned in Genesis and Ezekiel. In Christian theology, a cherub, often depicted in painting and sculpture as a beautiful, chubby, rosy-cheeked child with wings, is a member of the second order of angels in the celestial hierarchy. The word is also used of beautiful or innocent people, especially of children with sweet, innocent-looking faces.

chutzpah (1892), impudent self-confidence, nerve, or unmitigated gall, comes, via Yiddish **khutspa,** from Hebrew or Aramaic **hūspāh.**

hallelujah (1535) and **alleluia** (c. 1200), from Hebrew **hal alūyāh,** "Praise ye Yahweh," is a song of praise or thanksgiving to God, as well as an interjection used to express joy or thanks.

hosanna (c. 1000), an exclamation or cry used in praise of God, comes, via Greek **hosanna,** from Hebrew **hosh(i) ahnnā** "Save (us), we pray." According to the Gospels of Matthew,

Mark, and John, as Jesus entered Jerusalem, the pilgrims of Galilee greeted him with the word **hosanna,** in recognition of his messiahship.

jubilee (1382), comes from Hebrew **yōbhēl,** "ram, ram's horn, jubilee," since a ram's horn was used as a trumpet to proclaim the jubilee. In Leviticus 25, a jubilee was a yearlong period of emancipation and restoration observed by Jews once every fifty years. During the jubilee, Jewish slaves were given their freedom; lands in the open country or unwalled towns that had been sold were restored to the original owners or to their heirs; fields were left untilled; and all agricultural labors were suspended. A jubilee now signifies a special anniversary, such as the twenty-fifth (silver jubilee), fiftieth (golden), and sixtieth or seventy-fifth (diamond), or any season of celebration. In the Roman Catholic church, a jubilee is proclaimed by the pope every twenty-five years as a period of special solemnity.

kosher (1851), from Hebrew **kāshēr,** "right, fit, proper," is an adjective that signifies that something is sanctioned by Jewish dietary or ceremonial laws as being fit to be eaten or used. According to Talmudic and later law, certain animals (cattle, sheep, and fowl, for example) slaughtered in certain ritually prescribed ways are fit for consumption. If the proper ritual is not followed, the meat is deemed **trefa',** "unclean," and cannot be eaten. Informally, **kosher** means "genuine, legitimate, proper."

manna (c. 897), from Hebrew **mān hu,** "what is it?," is the name of the food miraculously supplied to the Israelites during their progress through the wilderness (in Exodus 16). Appearing as sweet round seeds in the morning dew, the manna was gathered before it melted in the heat of the sun. The word is commonly applied to any sudden or unexpected help or source of pleasure.

Sabbath (c. 950), the seventh day of the week, observed from Friday evening to Saturday evening as a day of rest and religious observance among Jews and some Christians, comes from Hebrew **shabbath,** "rest." Since the Reformation, the sabbath has also signified Sunday, "the Lord's day," observed by most Christians as a day of rest and worship in commemoration of the resurrection of Jesus Christ. From French, we have borrowed the word **sabbat,** "sabbath" (1652), which indicates a midnight meeting of witches, demons, and sorcerers held annually during the Middle Ages to celebrate the devil in rites and orgies. The expression **sabbatical year** originally signified a yearlong period of rest for the land observed every seventh year in ancient Judea. Today, it is applied to a year, usually every seventh, of break or change from one's normal routine, especially a year of release from teaching obligations granted to a professor for study or travel.

Seraph (plural **seraphim**) (c. 900), one of the heavenly beings flying above the throne of God in Isaiah's vision (Isaiah 6), comes from Hebrew **seraphim,** which, some scholars have suggested, may be related to the verb **sāraph,** "to burn (like lightning)", since the seraphim were especially distinguished by the ardor of their love (whereas the cherubim excelled in knowledge). Interestingly enough, the color red is often used in artistic representations of the seraphim. Other scholars maintain that the Hebrew **seraphim** is akin to Arabic **sharafa,** "to be lofty or illustrious." In the celestial hierarchy devised by the Pseudo-Dionysius, the seraphim were the highest of the nine orders of angels. Ranked highest to lowest, the cherubim were second; the thrones, third; dominions, fourth; virtues, fifth; powers, sixth; principalities, seventh; archangels, eighth; and angels, ninth and lowest.

Shibboleth (1382), a pet phrase, catchword, or slogan adopted by a sect or party, by which its followers may be distinguished, or a peculiarity of pronunciation, a custom, or a usage that is employed as a way to detect foreigners, or people from another district, comes from Hebrew **shibbōleth,** "stream in flood, freshet."

The word **shibboleth** was used by Jephthah and the Gileadites (in Judges 12) as a test by which to distinguish the fleeing Ephraimites, who could not pronounce the **sh,** from their own men. When an Ephraimite asked to cross the Jordan, the Gileadites asked him, "Are you an Ephraimite?" If he said no, they would retort, "Say 'shibboleth.'" When the Ephraimite said "sibboleth," they seized and killed him. The Bible records that forty-two thousand Ephraimites lost their lives at that time.

Hungarian

goulash (1866), a highly seasoned (especially with paprika) stew or ragout of beef or veal and vegetables, is borrowed from Hungarian **gulyas,** which is short for **gulyashus,** "herdsman's meat" (formed from **gulyas,** "herdsman," and **hus,** "meat"). **Goulash** is also a synonym for a hodgepodge, jumble, or mixture of heterogeneous elements. Since the 1920s, goulash has been used as a term in contract bridge to signify a round played with hands produced by a redeal or redistribution of unshuffled, previously dealt cards.

paprika (1896), a red, powdery condiment made from dried, finely ground ripe sweet peppers, is borrowed from Hungarian **paprika,** which was derived from Serbo-Croatian **papar,** "pepper."

Indic Languages

anaconda (1768), a large semiaquatic South American boa that frequently grows to a length of more than thirty feet, comes from Sinhalese (Singhalese) **henakandaya,** a kind of snake. Because of a mistake as to the geographic source of a specimen, scientists misapplied the name of a large snake in Sri Lanka to the large constricting snake of tropical South America, and the name has stuck. Anacondas seek their prey only at night and, contrary to popular belief, are not aggressive toward human beings.

avatar (1784), from Sanskrit **avatāra,** "a passing down," which is equivalent to **ava,** "down," and **-tāra,** "a passing over," is, in Hindu mythology, the descent of a divinity to the earth in an incarnate form. The Hindu god Vishnu was believed to have ten avatars, or incarnations: fish (his first avatar); tortoise (second); boar (third); half-man, half-lion (fourth); dwarf (fifth); Parasurama, the youngest son of a strict Brahmin hermit (sixth); the hero Rama (seventh); Krishna (eighth); Buddha (ninth); and himself riding a white horse named Kalki (his tenth and last avatar, which has yet to come). The word **avatar** also signifies an embodiment of a concept, attitude, or philosophy, usually in a person.

bandanna (1741), from Hindi **badhnu,** "tie-dying, cloth so dyed" (formed from the Sanskrit verb **badhnati,** "he ties"), is a large printed handkerchief, often with white spots and figures on a red or blue background. Bandannas were originally dyed by tying the cloth in different places, to prevent the parts from receiving the dye. The word now includes cotton handkerchiefs for the neck or head whose pattern has been produced by chemicals.

bangle (1787), from Hindi **bangli,** a variation of **bangri,** "glass ring, armlet," was originally a colored glass ring worn by women on their wrists. Today, the word denotes a decorative disk that hangs loosely (as on a bracelet or necklace) or a stiff, ring-shaped bracelet or anklet without a clasp that slips over the hand or foot, but occasionally with a hinged opening and a clasp.

beriberi (1703), from Sinhalese **beriberi,** a reduplication of **beri,** "weakness" to strengthen the sense of weakness, is a disease of the nerves, digestive system, and heart caused by a deficiency of vitamin B, or thiamine, in the diet. Beriberi is most common in the Far East, as the origin of its name would suggest. The earliest written record of beriberi is found in a Chinese medical book dating back to 2700 B.C. Still, it wasn't until the end of the nineteenth century that the cause of the disease was discovered. Beriberi is characterized by neuritis, numbness and tingling in the hands and feet, paralysis, vomiting, convulsions and severe emaciation or swelling of the body.

cheetah (1704), a long-legged, spotted, swift-moving cat of southwestern Asia and Africa resembling the leopard, comes from Hindi **cita,** which, in turn, was taken from Sanskrit **citraka,** "leopard," related to **citra,** "spotted, variegated, speckled." The cheetah has several doglike characteristics, and has often been tamed and trained for hunting deer and antelope in India. Cheetahs, the fastest of all four-legged animals, can attain speeds of seventy miles per hour in short spurts. Even when captured as adults, cheetahs can be tamed relatively easily. Tame cheetahs have been used in the United States to hunt coyotes.

chintz (1614), from Hindi, Mahrati, or Gujarati **chit,** all of which derive from Sanskrit **citra,** "variegated, spotted," is the name of a printed cotton fabric, typically glazed but sometimes unglazed, used especially for draperies and upholstery. The word has also been used of painted or stained calico imported from India. **Chintz** was originally spelled **chints** and began as a plural of singular **chint,** which was commonly used in English in the seventeenth century. Samuel Pepys, for example, in his diary entry for September 3, 1663, wrote: "Bought my wife a chint, that is, a painted Indian calico, for to line her new study." Chintz, deemed proper for draperies, was unacceptable in clothing worn in public. Although **chince** nightgowns were popular in England in the eighteenth century, women could not wear the fabric outdoors, as this news item from a 1768 issue of *Gentleman's Magazine* makes clear: "Two ladies were convicted before the Lord Mayor in the penalty of 5 pounds for wearing Chintz Gowns." **Chintz** is etymologically related to **cheetah,** the fastest land mammal.

Cot (1634), a light, collapsible bed, especially one of canvas stretched on a folding frame, comes from Hindi **khat,** "bedstead, couch, hammock, bier," which is ultimately derived from Sanskrit **khatva,** "bedstead, couch." The word is related to Tamil **kattil,** "bedstead."

dinghy (1794), from Bengali **dingi** or Hindi **dingī,** "little boat," the diminutive form of **dingā,** "boat, coasting vessel, sloop," is a small pleasure boat or light skiff. Originally denoting a rowing or sailing boat, resembling a canoe, used on Indian rivers to transport passengers and goods, the word was extended to lifeboats and tenders propelled by oars, sails, or motors and carried on larger boats. Today, **dinghy** is also used of rubber life rafts.

dungarees (1613), from Hindi **dungri,** the name of a kind of coarsely woven cloth, is a heavy, coarse, durable cotton twill, especially of blue denim, used in work clothes and overalls. Originally, **dungaree** was used to make sails and tents, but sailors, looking for a more durable, longer-lasting material to work in, fashioned the heavy fabric into clothes. Eventually, **dungarees** became the standard work uniform of both the U.S. Navy and the U.S. Marine Corps. Interestingly enough, the two words most often associated with dungarees, **denim** and **jeans,** are also derived from foreign languages. Both **denim** and **jeans** are, strictly speaking, toponyms—words derived from place names. **Denim** (1695) is short for French **serge de Nîmes** "serge of Nîmes," since Nîmes, a manufacturing town in southern France, turned out the heavy twilled cotton. The word **denim** first appears in English in a 1695 advertisement from the *Merchants Magazine* for "Serge Denims." And in 1703, the *London Gazette* featured "a pair of Flower'd Serge de Nim

Breeches." The word **jeans** (1495), also a toponym, is short for French **jean fustian,** which was earlier spelled **Gênes fustian,** "fustian of Genoa," since the Italian city of Genoa (called **Gênes** in France) also manufactured a sturdy twilled fabric, usually of cotton.

ginger (c. 1000), which comes, via Latin and Greek, from Sanskrit **srngavera** (formed from **srnga,** "horn," and **vera,** "body"), is a pungent aromatic rhizome that is used, dried and ground, as a spice in cooking and as medicine, and, preserved in syrup or candied, as a sweetmeat. **Ginger** is also the name of the reedlike plant native to the East Indies that grows up from the rhizome. **Ginger** is also a light sandy color and a synonym for pep and high spirits.

gunny (sack) (1711), a strong, coarse fabric usually of jute or hemp, used especially for bags or sacks, comes from Hindi **goni** (from Sanskrit **gona,** which has several meanings, including "ox," "a kind of grass," "sack," and "torn or ragged clothes").

juggernaut (1632), any large, overwhelming force or object that completely destroys everything in its path, is borrowed from Hindi **Jagannāth,** which is, in turn, derived from Sanskrit **Jagannātha,** "lord of the world" (formed from **jagat,** "world," and **nātha,** "lord"), a title of Krishna, the eighth avatar of the Hindu god Vishnu. **Jagannāth** specifically refers to a terrible idol of the god Vishnu at Puri in Orissa, India, which is annually drawn in procession on a huge cart, under whose wheels many devotees are said to have formerly thrown themselves to be crushed. **Juggernaut** is used of wars, battleships, and football teams, as well as of any institution or idea to which people blindly devote themselves. Richard Lester's 1974 suspense film *Juggernaut,* starring Omar Sharif and Richard Harris, is about a huge luxury liner that has received threats of being blown up if an enormous ransom is not paid. **Juggernaut** is related etymologically to **jaconet** (1769), a lightweight cotton cloth used to make bandages, clothing, and the lining of book spines, since **jaconet** is derived from Urdu **jagannath,** which is short for Jagannathpuri, a town in Orissa, India, where the cloth was originally manufactured. In England, juggernaut is also the name of a heavy truck, the **juggernaut lorry.**

j **ungle** (1776), a wild land overgrown with dense tropical vegetation, usually nearly impenetrable, a tangled mass of dense and luxuriant growth; or a place of violence and struggle for survival, as a huge industry, a prison, or an overpopulated city, is borrowed from Hindi **jangal,** "desert, waste." The Hindi word comes from Pali, Prakrit, or Sanskrit **jangala,** "dry, waterless desert." Thus, the meaning of **jungle** has undergone a fascinating change from a waterless desert to a tropical rain forest. In 1906, Upton Sinclair wrote a powerful novel attacking the meat-packing industry in Chicago. He called it *The Jungle.*

j **ute** (1746), a strong, coarse fiber used to make gunny sacks, burlap, canvas, and twine, comes from Bengali **jhuto** (derived from Sanskrit **juta,** "braid of hair"). Jute is obtained from the bark of two East Indian plants of the linden family. Jute was introduced into the United States in 1870, when the Department of Agriculture discovered that it could be grown successfully in the Gulf States from Texas to South Carolina.

k **arma** (1827), from Sanskrit **karman,** "act, deed," is, in Buddhism, the sum of a person's deeds in one of his successive lives, seen as determining his fate in the next—the cosmic principle according to which a person is rewarded or punished in one incarnation based on his or her actions in the previous incarnation. In Hinduism, karma is one of the ways of reaching Brahman. The word, then, also signifies necessary fate or destiny and, today, is used as a synonym for the good or bad vibrations felt to be emanating from someone or something.

loot (1788), goods, spoils, plunder taken by pillaging from an enemy or a captured city in war, is borrowed from Hindi **lut,** which is related to Sanskrit **loptra,** "booty, spoils," and **lunthati,** "he steals, he robs." Loot is now used of anything taken dishonestly or violently from another. It is also synonymous with a collection of articles of considerable value and is a slang expression for money.

mongoose (1698), from Marathi or Hindi **mangūs,** a derivative of Prakrit **manguso,** is an agile, ferret-size carnivore of India, related to the civet, that eats rodents, birds, and eggs, and is most famous for its ability to kill cobras and other venomous snakes. The mongoose is not immune to the cobra's venom, but it is protected by its fast reactions and by its dense, extremely strong hair. Mongooses were brought to Hawaii to control the rat and snake populations, but they destroyed so many small mammals and birds that importing them into the United States is now illegal.

nirvana (1836), from Sanskrit **nirvāna,** "blowing out, disappearance, extinction," which is related to the verb **nirvā,** "to blow," is the name given in Buddhism to the extinction of individual consciousness, to freedom from the endless cycle of reincarnations and absorption into the supreme spirit. It also signifies the extinction of all desires, passions, and illusions and the attainment of perfect happiness. Sigmund Freud viewed nirvana as the attraction felt by the psyche for a state of nonexistence and connected it with the death instinct. Today, **nirvana** is used of a blissful state marked by freedom from pain or worry.

pajamas (1800), a lightweight suit consisting of jacket and loose-fitting trousers adopted by Europeans for nightwear, similar to the loose, lightweight trousers of silk or cotton worn by both sexes in the Near East, is borrowed from Hindi or Urdu

pāyjāma, "leg garment" (from Persian **pāy**, "leg," and **jāma**, "clothing, garment"). Thus, etymologically speaking, the expression **pajama tops** is meaningless; **pajama bottoms**, redundant.

punch (1632), from Hindi **panch** (derived from Sanskrit **panca**, "five"), is a drink consisting of wine or spirits mixed with hot water or milk and flavored with sugar, lemons, and spices. Punch gets its name from the fact that originally it contained five ingredients. Punch is also the name of a beverage consisting of two or more fruit juices, sometimes carbonated. In the seventeenth century, one of the most popular punches was composed of brandy, lime juice, and water. Recently, the Bird's Eye Company brought out a fruit punch with the etymologically correct name of Five-Alive. The **punch** of fruit punch is not related to the punch that is delivered with the fist, or to the grotesque, humpbacked clown in the puppet show called "Punch [from **punchinello**] and Judy," or to the punch that makes holes in anything.

pundit (1672), from Hindi **pandit** (ultimately from Sanskrit **pandita**, "learned, skilled"), is a learned person, expert, or authority. The word also signifies a critic or commentator, one who makes comments or gives opinions in an authoritative manner. The original pundits (or pandits) were educated Hindus who were well versed in Sanskrit, philosophy, religion, and law. The pundit of the Indian Supreme Court was a Hindu law officer who functioned as an adviser to English judges, whose knowledge of Indian jurisprudence was often rudimentary. The office was eliminated in 1862.

Shampoo (1762), to wash the scalp or hair with a cleansing agent that leaves no filmy residue, to clean rugs and upholstery with a special preparation, is borrowed from Hindi **champo**, an inflected form of the verb **cāmpnā**, "to press, to knead (bread), to massage." The word is also used as a noun to signify both the act of shampooing and the preparation used. **Shampoo** was originally used in English as a synonym for "massage." Charles Dickens used the word in this sense in his 1848 novel *Dombey and Sons*: "Miss Pankey was shampooed every morning."

Swastika (1854), a cross with arms of equal length, each of which has a continuation at right angles, comes from Sanskrit **svastika,** "object conducive to well-being" (formed from **svasti,** "welfare, fortune, luck, success," and **-ka,** a noun suffix). Regarded as a good-luck symbol, the swastika appears as an ornament in the Old World and in America since prehistoric times. It is found on ancient Mesopotamian coinage; in early Christian and Byzantine art; in Hindu and Jain art in India; in China, Mycenae (in Greece), and the British Isles; and among the Mayas and Navajos. In 1910, the salutary symbolism of the swastika changed dramatically when a German poet and nationalist ideologist named Guido von List suggested it as an emblem for all anti-Semitic organizations. Nine years later, it was adopted as the official emblem of the National Socialist (Nazi) Party. And on September 15, 1935, the black swastika on a white circle against a crimson background became the national flag of Germany.

tom-tom (1693), a small-headed drum commonly played with the hands, comes from Hindi **tamtam,** an imitation of the sound of the instrument. The word also denotes a monotonous drumbeat or rhythm.

thug (ca. 1810), a violent ruffian or gangster, comes from the Hindi word **thug,** which, in turn, was derived from the Sanskrit **sthag,** "to hide, to conceal." The original thugs were members of a religious cult that flourished in India from the seventeenth to early nineteenth century. The thug cult, which attracted both Hindu and Muslim converts, worshiped the goddess Kali, the black earth-mother, whose rites included, at one time, the sacrificial killing of human beings. Kali was depicted with dark skin; a bloodstained, tusked face; and a brow bearing a third eye. Her body was naked except for earrings made of little children, a necklace of snakes, a necklace of skulls, and a belt adorned with demons' hands. According to a myth that justified the practices of Thuggee, the thug way of life, Kali attempted to prevent the annihilation of mankind by killing a monster named Rukt Bij-dana, who devoured the first men as soon as they were created. Since a new monster sprang forth from each drop of blood shed by Rukt Bij-dana, Kali created two men, to whom she entrusted her **rumal,** or handkerchief, symbol of the task of strangulation, which she imposed upon them. When the two had successfully destroyed all the demons and offered to return the handkerchief to Kali, she commanded them and all their descendants to murder any men not related to them. Thus, the brutal acts committed by the thugs—the robbing, strangling, poisoning, and burying alive of innocent victims—were viewed as acts of worship. Indeed, the tortures were often prolonged so that Kali might derive greater pleasure.

Veranda (1711), a large open porch or roofed gallery attached to the exterior of a building, partly enclosed by a railing and often erected as a protection or shelter from the sun and rain, is borrowed from Hindi **varanda,** which may have come from Portuguese **varanda** or from Bengali **baranda** (from Persian **bar amadah,** "coming out").

Italian

antic (1529), a playful prank, a funny trick, or caper, or an adjective meaning "funny," "frolicsome," or "ludicrous," comes from Italian **antico,** "ancient," which apparently originally meant "grotesque," and was first used to describe the fantastic representations of human, animal, and vegetative forms that appeared in Roman ruins. The figures, usually running into one another somewhat incongruously, were discovered by archaeologists digging up various ancient sites in Rome, as the Baths of Titus. The word was soon extended to anything grotesque or bizarre. For example, in the sixteenth century, the word denoted a buffoon, a clown, or any performer playing a ludicrous part in a play. In Shakespeare's play *Richard II*, King Richard describes death as an **antick** who "within the hollow crown that rounds the mortal temples of a king . . . sits . . . scoffing his state, and grinning at his pomp."

balcony (1618), from Italian **balcone,** "balcony, full-length window" (which originally meant "scaffold" in Old Italian), is a kind of elevated platform projecting from the wall of a house or room. Balconies are usually enclosed by a balustrade or railed; hence the application of the term to a balustraded projecting gallery in a theater.

ballot (1549), a slip or sheet of paper or cardboard on which a voter records his or her vote, comes from Italian **ballotta,** "a little ball, a little round bullet." Ballots were originally small balls, used for secret voting, dropped into a box or other receptacle. A white ball indicated a yes, while a black ball meant no. Eventually, ballots were made of paper. The word now extends to one's right to vote and to the list of candidates to be voted on. The verb **blackball** (1770), meaning "to ostracize, to exclude socially," refers to the practice of having members of a private club vote on candidates by placing colored balls into a box. If the box contained white (or red) balls when the voting ended, the candidate was welcomed as a new member of the club. A single black ball, on the other hand, was sufficient to exclude him.

bandit (1591), a member of a band of marauders, an outlaw who lives by plunder, a highwayman, comes from Italian **bandito,** "outlaw, exile, proscribed one," which is the past participle of **bandire,** "to exile, to banish, to announce publicly." One of the earliest, if not the earliest, to use the word in English was William Shakespeare. In his 1591 *Second Part of King Henry the Sixth*, the duke of Suffolk says, "A Roman sworder and banditto slave / Murder'd sweet Tully; Brutus' bastard hand / Stabb'd Julius Caesar; savage islanders / Pompey the Great; and Suffolk dies by pirates."

bordello (1598), another name for a brothel or house of prostitution, is borrowed from Italian **bordello,** which, in turn, was derived from Old French **bordel,** "cabin, wooden hut." In 1386, Chaucer used the French word: "Harlottis, that haunten bordels of these foule wommen." The Italian word first appears in English in Ben Jonson's 1598 comedy *Every Man in His Humor,* when old Kno'well reads a letter addressed to his son and comments: "From the Bordello it might come as well, The Spittle, or Pict-hatch."

broccoli (1699), from the Italian plural of **broccolo,** "little cabbage sprout," itself a diminutive of **brocco,** "sprout, nail, shoot, stalk," is a cultivated form of cabbage whose leafy stalks and clusters of green or purple florets are eaten as a vegetable. The first citation in English occurs in Evelyn's *Acetaria* in 1699—a reference to broccoli from Naples.

bronze (1739), an alloy consisting largely of copper and tin, is borrowed, via French, from Italian **bronzo,** "brass, bell-metal" (which is perhaps related to **bruno,** "brown"). Bronze was one of the first alloys made by humans, and was probably discovered as a result of smelting copper ore that contained tin as an impurity. Although bronze is believed to date back to the fourth millennium B.C., it was not commonly used until about 2500 B.C. The term **Bronze Age,** coined in the 1860s, designates a period in the history of human culture, following the Stone Age and preceding the Iron Age, during which bronze weapons and implements were used. Numismatists use the word **bronze** to identify coins made of bronze, especially those from the Roman Empire. A work of art, such as a statue, statuette, or bust is often referred to as a **bronze.**

buffoon (1585), a coarse and usually ill-educated person who is given to undignified jesting, or a clownish individual who amuses others by tricks and jokes, is borrowed, via French, from Italian **buffone,** "one who puffs up his cheeks, big puff of breath," related to the verb **buffare,** "to puff up."

cameo (fifteenth century), from Italian **cam(m)eo,** is a precious stone having two layers of different colors, on the upper of which a figure is carved in relief, while the lower serves as a contrasting background. Cameo cutting is believed to have begun in the Middle East. It flourished in classical Rome, during the Renaissance, in the baroque seventeenth century, and enjoyed a magnificent revival in the late eighteenth and early nineteenth centuries. The ancients used onyx, agate, and especially sardonyx, a variety of chalcedony composed of alternate parallel layers of white and red chalcedony. The last great specialist in this medium was an Italian, Benedetto Pistrucci (1784–1855), who lived in England. The word **cameo** is also used of minor parts in motion pictures played by well-known actors and often limited to a single scene. Examples of cameo roles include Bette Davis as Catherine the Great in the 1959 biopic *John Paul Jones,* Laurence Olivier as Mr. Creakle in the 1970 *David Copperfield,* Buster Keaton in *Sunset Boulevard,* and Kevin McCarthy in the 1978 remake of *Invasion of the Body Snatchers,* as well as Marlene Dietrich as a San Francisco saloon hostess, Ronald Colman as a railroad official in India, and Bea Lillie as a London revivalist in the 1956 cameo-studded *Around the World in 80 Days.*

canteen (1737), which comes, via French **cantine,** "bottle case, sutler's shop," from Italian **cantina,** "wine cellar, cave," is the name of a small flask used especially by soldiers and hikers for carrying water and other liquids. It is also applied to the cafeteria and general store at a military base, to a social club or recreation center where free entertainment is provided for military personnel or a community's teenagers, and to a snack bar. In Great Britain, a canteen is a chest for storing silverware.

Cappuccino (1948), a hot (or iced) beverage consisting of espresso coffee and frothed hot milk or cream, often flavored with powdered cinnamon and topped with whipped cream, comes from Italian **cappuccino,** "Capuchin," from the resemblance of the drink's color to that of a Capuchin monk's habit. The Order of Friars Minor Capuchin was founded in 1529 as an austere branch of the Franciscan order. Like the Jesuits, the Capuchins felt that their special mission was to check the advance of Protestantism in Europe and reclaim lands that had been lost to the Roman Catholic faith. In the United States, cappuccino seems to have first become popular in San Francisco.

Carnival (1549), a traveling amusement show with sideshows and rides, or any season or festival of entertainment or masquerading, such as a winter carnival, comes from Italian **carnevale,** an alteration of Old Italian **carnelevale,** "removal of meat" (formed from **carne,** "flesh, meat," and **levare,** "to put away, to remove"). Originally, carnival was the season of merrymaking and revelry that immediately preceded Lent. Since Lent ushered in a period of fasting and abstinence from meat, the days immediately preceding Ash Wednesday, and especially Shrove Tuesday itself, were devoted to riotous amusement and the conspicuous consumption of food. In France, Shrove Tuesday was called Mardi Gras ("Fat Tuesday") and was observed with parades and festivities. There is also a popular (if spurious) etymology of **carnival** from **carne, vale,** "goodbye, meat!"

Carousel (1650), a merry-go-round in an amusement park or a continuously revolving belt or conveyer on which objects are placed, such as the luggage carousel at an airport, comes, via French **car(r)ousel,** "joust, tournament," from Italian **carosello,** "a kind of ball game." The game, played with clay balls, originated in Naples, where it was called **carusello,** since the balls resembled tiny bald heads (**caruso** being the word for "shorn head"). Today, photographic transparencies are held in a rotating tray called a carousel before being lowered through slots into a projector for viewing.

Cartoon (1671), from Italian **cartone,** "pasteboard, stout paper, cartoon," originally indicated a full-scale drawing on heavy paper made as a design for a painting to be transferred to a fresco, tapestry, canvas, mosaic, or stained glass. In the nineteenth century, the word was extended to sketches and drawings, often humorous, in newspapers and periodicals, intended as satire or caricature. Today, the word is frequently synonymous with **comic strip.** As early as 3000 B.C., Egyptian artists drew amusing cartoons of animals on papyrus. The modern cartoon probably originated with Wilhelm Busch's *Max und Moritz* (1870), a story about two mischievous boys, which was translated into English by Charles T. Brooks, a Boston clergyman, and published in comic book form in the United States. It greatly influenced Rudolph Dirks, who based *The Katzenjammer Kids* (begun in 1896) on it. Some of the earliest comic strips include James Swinnerton's *Little Bears* (1892), which featured the first continuing characters to appear in a daily newspaper (William Randolph Hearst's San Francisco *Examiner*); Richard Outcault's *Yellow Kid* (in 1895) and *Buster Brown* (in 1897); Bud Fisher's *Mutt and Jeff* (1907); and George McManus's *Bringing Up Father* (1912), which featured Maggie and Jiggs, probably the two most popular comic strip characters of all times.

Cascade (1641), from Italian **cascata** (derived from the verb **cascare,** "to fall"), via French **cascade,** is a steep waterfall or a series of shallow or steplike waterfalls. It is also applied to anything that resembles a waterfall, especially something that falls or rushes forth in quantity, like a cascade of coins. **Cascade,** used as a verb, was once deemed colloquial to the point of vulgarity. It was the eighteenth- and nineteenth-century equivalent of today's **upchuck** or **barf.** In Tobias Smollett's 1771 novel *Humphry Clinker,* Jery Melford reveals, rather indelicately, to his collegemate Watkin Phillips that Mrs. Tabitha Bramble "cascaded" into an urn.

Casino (1789), from Italian **casino,** "little house," is a building or large room for social amusement, especially gambling. Casinos were originally public buildings equipped with dance floors and music. Gambling games were soon introduced, and gradually the word began to be used as a synonym for gambling house. In Italy, the word is often used of summerhouses and lodges. Casino is also the name of a card game in which players win cards by matching or combining the cards in their hands with those lying faceup on the table.

Charlatan (1611), from Italian **ciarlatano,** "babbler, chatterer," via French **charlatan,** is a person who pretends to have more ability or knowledge than he or she actually possesses, a quack, impostor, fraud, or phony. Ben Jonson used the Italian form of the word in his 1605 comedy *Volpone*: "Ciarlitani that spread their cloaks on the pavement." In 1854, Lady Lytton used the more common, French form when she wrote, rather unflatteringly, in her *Behind Scenes*, of the author of *Tristram Shandy*: "The charlatanic shade of that great petty larcener of sentiment, Laurence Sterne."

Confetti (1815) are small bits or streamers of paper, usually brightly colored, thrown or dropped from a height to increase the merriment of a festive occasion, such as a wedding, birthday, New Year's Eve or Mardi Gras party. The word **confetti** is the plural of Italian **confetto,** "sweetmeat, confection," since sweetmeats made of fruits preserved with sugar, as well as small oval masses of sugar (often enclosing caraway seeds and almonds), were originally flung from balconies during carnival in Italy. Eventually, the candied conserves were replaced by tiny balls, the size of marbles, made of soft white plaster thrown by revelers in each other's faces and stuffed down their shirts. These, in turn, gave way, especially in England, to small disks of colored paper hurled (instead of rice) at the bride and groom at weddings.

Contraband (1529), goods prohibited by law from being imported or exported, illegal traffic in goods, or smuggling, comes, via Spanish **contrabanda** or French **contrabande,** from Italian **contrabando** (now **contrabbando**), which is ultimately derived from Latin **contra,** "against," and **bannum,** "proclamation, ban, statute." During the American Civil War, the word **contra-band** referred specifically to a black slave who was brought or managed to escape to the North (or to somewhere within the Union lines).

Credenza (1880), from Italian, is a side table or sideboard on which dishes are placed before they are served at table. Credenzas are related, etymologically, to the small credence tables, or credences, of Roman Catholic and Anglican churches, on which the eucharistic elements are placed previous to the Consecration of the Mass. Both **credenza** and **credence** are derived from the Latin root **cred-,** which means "to believe." Whereas the oblations placed on a credence table are regarded by the faithful as objects of belief or faith, the offerings placed on the original credenzas in noble Italian households during the Renaissance were consigned there as a precaution against poisoning, in an age when being poisoned by one's host was a not uncommon adjunct of dining out. The first credenzas were, then, testing tables where foods were tasted by servants to assure guests they were safe to eat.

dilettante (1748), from Italian **dilettante,** "one who takes delight" (noun use of the present participle of Italian **dilet-tare,** "to delight"), is a person who takes up an art, science, or activity just for amusement and without serious aim. **Dilettante** is a derogatory term applied to amateurs and dabblers whose interest in a subject is superficial. The English dramatist Samuel Foote (1720–1777), more famous for losing a leg as a result of a practical joke and exploiting his disability in a farce than for any of his comedies or satirical skits, had a character in his 1770 play *The Lame Lover* remark: "Frederick is a bit of Macaroni and adores the soft Italian termination in **a. . . .** Yes, a delitanti all over." Seventy years later, Thomas Macauley (1800–1859) wrote in one of his essays: "The Dilettante sneered at their want of taste. The Maccaroni blackballed them as vulgar fellows."

ditto (1678), from Italian **ditto,** a variation of **detto,** "said," is etymologically the Italian equivalent of the Latin word **dictum.** It signifies something previously mentioned, and is synonymous with "the aforesaid" or "the same" (used in lists to avoid repetition). A ditto is also a duplicate copy made on a Ditto machine, the name **Ditto** being a trademark.

fiasco (1855), a complete failure or a bulbous, long-necked bottle for wine, encased in a woven straw or raffia basket enabling the bottle to stand upright, comes from Italian **fiasco,** "flask, bottle." **Fiasco,** meaning ignominious flop, disaster, or catastrophe, comes from the Italian expression **far fiasco,** "to make a bottle." Italian etymologists have proposed various theories and alleged incidents in Italian theatrical history to explain why making a bottle would signify failing utterly. But perhaps it is the round-bottomed shape of the fiasco itself and its inability to stand without its protective straw covering that best explains the idiomatic sense—any respectable glassblower would be completely embarrassed to admit making a bottle that was unable to stand.

ghetto (1611), the quarter of a city in which Jews were required to live, comes from **ghetto,** which may have been an abbreviation of **borghetto,** the diminutive form of **borgo,** "borough." Others suggest that the Italian word was derived from Hebrew **get,** "divorce," and thus implies separation. Still others maintain that **ghetto** is related to the verb **ghettare,** "to throw." The first ghetto was an island near Venice to which Jews were restricted in 1516. Later, the word was applied to any of the segregated areas of Jewish habitation throughout Europe—areas sometimes surrounded by walls, the gates of which were locked at night. Today, the word signifies a heavily populated slum, inhabited largely by members of an ethnic minority.

graffiti (1851), the plural of Italian **graffito,** "scratching, scribbling," is a drawing, inscription, or scrawl scratched on a wall, bench, or other surface. Originally scratched on the ancient walls, doorposts, and pillars of Pompeii and in Roman catacombs, graffiti were the work of idlers—schoolboys, slaves, and loafers. Roman graffiti were of various types—witty doggerel verses, insulting caricatures, amatory effusions, obscene propositions, advertisements of plays, and political endorsements. For example, there is the indecent "I am yours—for two asses," an **as** being a small copper coin worth less than a nickel. And there are some that allude to athletic and gladiatorial games, such as "EPAPHRA PILICREPVS NON ES," or "Epaphras, you aren't (much of) a ballplayer." Today, graffiti are often spray-painted or scratched on sidewalks, apartment buildings, and subway cars, and in public restrooms.

granite (1646), from Italian **granito,** "grained, grainy," is a grainy crystalline rock of varying color consisting essentially of quartz, mica, and orthoclase feldspar, used especially for building and for monuments. **Granite** (from Italian **granita**) has also been used in the United States to indicate a kind of rough-grained water-ice or sherbet. New Hampshire, because of the abundance of the rock found there, is called the Granite State.

grotto (1617), a cave or cavern, or an excavation or structure, often adorned with oyster shells, made to resemble a rocky cave, is borrowed from Italian **grotta** (although Dante has **grotto**), which comes, via Latin **crupta,** "subterranean passage, chamber," from Greek **krypte,** "hidden place."

gusto (1620), from Italian or possibly Spanish **gusto,** "taste," signifies hearty relish or keen enjoyment, enthusiasm, or fondness. In 1647, an English writer named Boyle wrote about the addictive properties of tobacco: "which tho' at first sucked in with reluctance barely to please the company, men afterwards find a gusto in, and are unable to leave off."

i ncognito (1649), having one's identity concealed or unavowed, comes from Italian **incognito,** "unknown" (ultimately from Latin **incognitus**). The word was used especially in reference to royalty who used to conceal their identity so as not to be openly recognized. William Wyler's captivating 1953 film *Roman Holiday* is a cinematic delight about a newspaperman (Gregory Peck) who falls for a lonely princess traveling incognito (Audrey Hepburn, who won an Academy Award for her brilliant performance). The female **incognita,** a woman or girl traveling incognito, entered the English language in the seventeenth century, but is now pretty much obsolete.

i nferno (1834), hell or a place of torment and misery that re- sembles hell, comes from Italian **inferno,** "hell" (from Latin **infernus,** "situated below, pertaining to the underworld"). When capitalized and in italics, *Inferno* refers to the first part of Dante's masterpiece *The Divine Comedy,* depicting hell and the suffering of the damned. **Inferno** has been used in the title of several motion pictures, including *Dante's Inferno* (1935, starring Spencer Tracy and Claire Trevor), which features a hot, sultry Spanish dance per- formed by Rita Cansino, who later became Rita Hayworth; *Inferno* (1953, starring Robert Ryan and Rhonda Fleming), about a pair of ruthless lovers who plot to abandon the woman's millionaire hus- band in the Mojave Desert; and *The Towering Inferno* (1974, starring Paul Newman and Steve McQueen), about a fire in one of the world's tallest buildings.

i nfluenza (1743), an acute infectious viral disease of the res- piratory tract, comes from Italian, meaning "a flowing onto." A doublet of the word **influence,** the word originally had astrolog- ical significance. Like many astrologers today, those who lived in eighteenth-century Italy believed that the activities and destinies of human beings were controlled by the stars and planets, whose mys- terious power "flowed onto" them. The planets were thought to control certain diseases, especially those that affected the throat and bronchial tubes. Early Italian doctors, unable to explain satisfactorily the causes of influenza or its method of transmission, and even less able to prescribe effective remedies against it, simply called it **influenza,** attributing epidemic outbreaks of the disease to the agency of hostile stars and planets. The two most deadly outbreaks of the disease in modern times were the influenza pandemic of 1918–1919, in which the deaths numbered in the millions, and the Asian flu epidemic of 1957, whose death figures rose into the thousands.

i**solate** (1807), to set apart, detach, or separate from others, comes from Italian **isolato,** "made into an island" (formed from **isola,** "island"). **Isolate** is etymologically related to **insulate** (derived from Latin **insulatus,** "made into an island," which comes from Latin **insula,** "island"). In medicine, doctors isolate, or quarantine, an infected person from contact with noninfected persons. In medical laboratories, isolation consists of separating one substance from another substance so as to keep it pure or in a free state. In linguistics, an isolated language is one with no demonstrable relationship to other languages, as Basque and Ainu.

l**agoon** (1612), from Italian **laguna,** which is derived, in turn, from Latin **lacuna** "pool, ditch, hole, gap, lake," is a shallow sound, channel, or pond separated from a larger body of water by sandbanks. **Lagoon** also signifies an artificial pond or pool for the processing and storage of sewage and industrial waste. On muddy islands in the center of one of the world's largest lagoons (it covers an area of 180 square miles), early fishermen sank oak piles from which would arise the glorious city of Venice.

l**ava** (1750), the fluid or semifluid molten rock that issues from a volcano or volcanic vent, comes from Italian **lava,** which is probably derived from Latin **labes,** "a sliding down, falling," rather than from the Latin verb **lavare,** "to wash," even though Neapolitans used the word to refer to streams suddenly caused by rain.

libretto (1742), from Italian **libretto,** "little book," is the text or words of a vocal work, usually an opera, for the musical theater. The word first appears in English in Samuel Richardson's 1742 novel *Pamela*: "If the Libretto, as they call it, is not approved, the Opera . . . will be condemned." The first libretto published in the United States (in 1767 in New York City) contained the text not of a famous Italian opera but of a now forgotten two-act comic opera called *The Disappointment, or The Force of Credulity.* Composed by a similarly forgotten composer, Andrew Barton, the satirical work concerned treasure supposedly buried by Blackbeard the Pirate.

macaroni (1599), from Italian **maccheroni,** the plural of **maccherone,** "dumpling, macaroni," is pasta made of semolina shaped into long, slender tubes. Some scholars have suggested that the Italians (via the Romans) borrowed the Greek word **makaria,** "blessed," which was used to describe a sacrificial cake made out of a mixture of broth and barley. For the Italians, then, the word signified a kind of hodgepodge, a heterogeneous mixture. This sense is still present in the English adjective **macaronic,** a linguistic term used to denote a mixture of vernacular words with Latin words, or non-Latin words having Latin endings. And it is even more true of the tube-shaped pasta served with all kinds of sauces. Once taken into English, besides meaning "pasta in the form of dried, hollow tubes" served with different sauces, the word also came to mean a dandy or coxcomb, an Englishman who affected Continental mannerisms and wore clothes that were fashionable among the Continental elite. In the eighteenth century, the Macaroni Club was founded in London, its name probably adopted to indicate the preference of the club's members for foreign cuisine, macaroni especially, which was not commonly eaten in England at that time. An article in a 1770 issue of the *Oxford Magazine* paints a decidedly unflattering portrait of a Macaroni: "There is indeed a kind of animal, neither male nor female, a thing of the neuter gender, lately started up amongst us. It is called a Macaroni. It talks without meaning, it smiles without pleasantry, it eats without appetite, it rides without exercise, it wenches without passion." A certain Madame D'Arblay records in her diary that it was the custom of these Macaronis to wear two watches. And Hugh Walpole says that the Macaroni Club is composed of "travelled young men who wear long curls and spying glasses." The sense of **macaroni** as elegant fop figures importantly in "Yankee Doodle Dandy," a mocking song sung by British soldiers to make fun of the poorly dressed colonists. So shabby were the clothes they fought in, the song suggests, that when the Yankee Doodle Dandy "stuck a feather in his cap," he "called it macaroni." There was, incidentally, a militia from Maryland during the Revolutionary War who were known as the Macaronies because they wore splendid uniforms otherwise unknown in the colonies.

m **acaroon** (1611), a small cookie made of ground almonds (and sometimes coconut), egg whites, and sugar, is derived from Italian **maccheroni.** The original English macaroons were fritterlike buns made from sugar, almonds, and rosewater. In the eighteenth century, **macaroon** was, for a while, synonymous with **macaroni.**

m **adrigal** (1588), from Italian **madrigale** (ultimately derived from Latin **matricalis,** "simple, pertaining to the womb"), is a secular song without instrumental accompaniment, usually for four to six voices, that was extremely popular in the sixteenth and seventeenth centuries. The madrigal, with its rich polyphonic style, was especially cultivated by Flemish, Italian, and English composers. A **madrigal comedy** or **madrigal opera** is an entire play set to music in the form of madrigals, the most famous of which is Orazio Vecchi's *Amfiparnaso,* composed in 1594. It consists of three acts and a prologue, and its characters are the stock figures of the commedia dell'arte. Madrigal is also the name given to a short lyrical poem dealing with love and able to be set to music.

M **afia** (1875), from Italian (Sicilian) **maffia,** "elegance, bravura, courage," is the name of a nineteenth-century Sicilian secret terrorist society, like the Camorra in Naples, that showed its contempt of the government and the law by committing criminal acts. It continues today—a hierarchically structured organization allegedly engaged in racketeering, drug trafficking, smuggling, and gambling in the United States, Italy, and elsewhere. A **mafia** is any small group of people with similar interests who are influential in an organization or field. Some linguists suggest that the word **maffia** was borrowed by the Sicilians from Arabic **mahyah,** "boastful, bragging." There is even an ingenious, if implausible, theory that the word **mafia** was originally an acronym for "**M**orte **a**lla **F**rancia **I**talia **A**nela," or "Death to France Is the Cry of Italy." A **mafioso** (1875) is a member of the Mafia (or of a mafia).

malaria (1740), from Italian **mala aria,** "bad air," is a human disease caused by a parasitic protozoan in the red blood cells, which is transmitted by the bite of anopheles mosquitoes. Medieval Italian scientists originally believed that the disease, which is characterized by periodic attacks of chills, fever, and profuse sweating, was due to the unwholesome condition of the atmosphere (or air) in humid, swampy regions; hence the name **malaria.** The actual cause of malaria was not discovered until 1880, when a French army doctor stationed in Algeria, Charles Laveran, noted unusual shapes in the red blood cells of malaria patients. Seventeen years later, a British army physician, Ronald Ross, proved conclusively that mosquitoes transmitted the disease.

manifesto (1644), a public declaration of intentions, views, or motives, issued by governments, rulers, individuals, or organizations, comes from Italian **manifesto,** "denunciation, manifest," derived ultimately from Latin **manifestus,** "evident, visible, palpable, disclosed."

mezzanine (1711), from Italian **mezzanino,** "little middle," a diminutive of **mezzano,** "middle," is, in a theater, the lowest balcony (or the first few rows of such a balcony). In a building, a mezzanine is a low-ceilinged story between stories of greater height, especially between the ground floor and the story above, but sometimes between the ground floor and the basement level.

miniature (1586), from Italian **miniatura,** "miniature painting," is a representation or copy of something on a small or reduced scale. It is also applied to paintings in illuminated manuscripts or to small paintings, especially portraits, on ivory, metal, or vellum. Some linguists assert that the Italian word **miniatura** comes from Latin **minium,** "cinnabar, red lead," since it was used in the art of illuminating manuscripts. In 1697, John Dryden wrote in the dedication of his translation of Virgil's *Aeneid:* "Tragedy is the miniature of human life; an epic poem is the draught at length."

motto (1589), a short sentence, phrase, or maxim inscribed on an object (as, for example, a scroll, crest, or shield) or adopted as the guiding principle of a person, team, school, organization, state, and so forth, comes from Italian **motto** (derived from Latin **muttum,** "sound, utterance," and related to the French **mot,** "word"). The motto of the United States, "In God we trust," which originated during the Civil War as an inscription for U.S. coins, was finally designated as the national motto by Congress in 1956. Some of the more well-known state mottoes are: "We dare defend our rights" (Alabama); "Ad astra per aspera," or "To the stars through difficulties" (Kansas); "United we stand, divided we fall" (Kentucky); "Esse quam videri," or "To be rather than to seem" (North Carolina); "Dum spiro spero," or "While I breathe, I hope" (South Carolina); and the intriguing "Montani semper liberi," or "Mountaineers are always free" (West Virginia).

mountebank (1577), a person who sells quack medicines from an elevated platform, appealing to his audience by means of stories, tricks, and juggling, comes from Italian **montimbanco,** "one who climbs on a bench," formed from **mont(are),** "to climb, to mount," and **im,** "onto," and **banco,** "bench." The word has been extended to a charlatan or boastful pretender to skill or knowledge.

Opera (1644), from Italian **opera,** "work, opera" (formed from the plural of Latin **opus,** "labor, work, service"), is an extended dramatic composition in which music forms an integral part. An opera, sung to instrumental accompaniment, includes recitatives, arias, choruses, and sometimes ballet. Developed in Florence at the end of the sixteenth century, the earliest operas were *Dafne,* poem by Rinuccini, music by J. Peri (1597); *Euridice,* poem by Rinuccini, music by G. Caccini (1602); and *Euridice,* poem by Rinuccini, music by Peri and Caccini (1600). The first major work in the history of opera was Monteverdi's *La favola d'Orfeo* (1607). John Evelyn (1620–1706), a friend of renowned diarist Samuel Pepys and an expert on gardening, first mentioned the word in his diary, when describing his travels abroad.

Operetta (1770), a short opera, usually light and humorous, is borrowed from Italian **operetta,** "little opera." The modern operetta originated in Vienna with Franz von Suppe, who composed about thirty operettas, and in Paris with Jacques Offenbach, who wrote about ninety. Johann Strauss the Younger perfected the Viennese operetta, and his work *Die Fledermaus,* composed in 1874, has remained popular to the present day. In the United States, the most important composers of operettas were Victor Herbert, Rudolf Friml, and Sigmund Romberg.

Parapet (1583), from Italian **parapetto,** "a defense breast-high," formed from **para,** "(guard) against," and **petto,** "chest, breast," is a defensive wall or rampart of stone or earth to protect soldiers, or a low wall or railing at the edge of a balcony, pier, roof, quay, or bridge to prevent people from falling over.

parasol (1616), a lightweight umbrella carried especially by women in the West (and by persons of high rank in the East) as a sunshade, comes, via French **parasol,** from Italian **parasole,** formed from **para,** "(guard) against," and **sole,** "sun." The **parasol ant** is a leaf-carrying ant of South America; **parasol pine** is another name for the stone pine; the **parasol mushroom** is a species of mushroom with a broad reddish brown pileus.

piano (1767), a musical instrument in which felt-covered hammers operated from a keyboard strike steel wire strings, comes from Italian **piano,** which is short for **pianoforte** (from **piano,** "soft," and **forte,** "loud"), and was so called because its tones could be varied in loudness. The piano, originally called **gravicembalo col piano e forte,** was invented by Bartolommeo Cristofori in 1709. It was basically a harpsichord equipped with hammers and a mechanism capable of playing loud and soft by changing the force of attack on the keys. The first mention of the word in English occurs in the *Playbill of the Theatre Royal at Covent Garden* for May 16, 1767: "At the end of Act I, Miss Brickler will sing a favourite song from 'Judith,' accompanied by Mr. Dibdin, on a new instrument, called Piano Forte."

pizza (1935), a flat, open-faced pie made of thinly rolled bread dough topped with tomato sauce and cheese, and sometimes garnished with sausage, meatball, or pepperoni slices, mushrooms, olives, or anchovies, and baked in a very hot oven, comes from Italian **pizza,** whose origin is obscure. It may ultimately come, like **pesto,** from a word that means "to pound, to beat" (such as Latin **pinsere**), or it may be derived from Greek **petea,** "bran." **Pizzeria** (1943), formed from Italian **pizza** and **-eria,** a suffix signifying a place or establishment, is a restaurant or bakery where pizzas are made, sold, and eaten. There is a lot of disagreement about the first pizzas and pizzerias in the United States. According to some, the first pizzeria was opened by Gennaro Lombardi, on Spring Street in New York City, in 1905. It was not, however, until a quarter of a century later that Lombardi added tables, chairs, and silverware. Still, since pizza was considered immigrant food, the word was seldom used. But during World War II, Americans began to acquire a taste for pizza, which led to the proliferation of pizzerias in the late 1940s. There are those who believe that pizza, as we now know it, originated in New Haven, Connecticut, in 1925, when a native Italian baker named Frank Pepe rented a small bakery on Wooster Street. There, he made simple pizzas with crushed tomatoes and grated cheese. After selling his pies for many years from a horsedrawn cart, Frank Pepe bought a building next to his bakery and opened the Pizzeria Napoletana in 1934. Pepe's was the first pizzeria in New Haven, if not in the United States, and is still reputed, together with New Haven's Sally's and The Spot, to serve the best pizzas in America.

portfolio (1722), from Italian **portafoglio** (formed from **portare,** "to carry," and **foglio,** "leaf, sheet of paper"), is a flat, portable case for carrying loose sheets of paper, prints, pamphlets, maps, or official documents of state. A portfolio also represents the total holdings of the securities of a private investor or the commercial paper of a financial institution. An artist's **portfolio** is a set of drawings or photographs carried loose in a folder or bound together as a book.

presto (1683), from Italian **presto,** "quick(ly)," is a direction used to indicate the fastest speeds in music. **Presto** is faster than allegro. **Prestissimo** (c. 1724) indicates the fastest possible speed. **Presto** is also a word used by magicians to emphasize the amazing rapidity with which a particular trick has been completed.

quarantine (1609), from Italian **quarantina** (derived, via French and Venetian dialect, from Latin **quadraginta,** "forty"), signifies a period of strict isolation imposed to prevent the spread of disease. **Quarantine** gets its name from the fact that the period of detention or isolation imposed on ships, persons, animals, or plants suspected of carrying contagious disease or pests was originally forty days. After forty days, it was believed, the possibility of spreading the disease effectively vanished. The practice of restricting cargo, passengers, and crew originated in the fourteenth century (at Ragusa on the Dalmatian coast of the Adriatic Sea) during the bubonic plague, or Black Death. Restrictions at Venice were particularly stringent. Actually, the length of the very first quarantine was thirty days, not forty days, but when it was discovered that a month was not sufficient to destroy the infection, the period was lengthened to the forty days that have given **quarantine** its name. Today, the World Health Organization lists four quarantinable diseases: cholera, plague, smallpox, and yellow fever. The word **quarantine** was first used in English, however, as a legal term indicating the period of forty days during which a widow was allowed to remain in the chief manor house of her dead husband.

regatta (1652), a boat race, as, for example, of rowboats, speedboats, yachts, or sailboats, comes from Upper Italian (Venetian) **regatta,** "strife, contention," the name given in Venice to gondola races held on the Grand Canal. The first English regatta took place on the Thames on June 23, 1775.

Scenario (1878), from Italian **scenario** (ultimately from Latin **scenarium** and **scaena,** "stage, background"), is an outline or synopsis of the plot of a play; the outline of a motion picture or television show, giving descriptions of scenes and characters; a screenplay; or a shooting script. A scenario is also an imagined sequence of events, especially of a projected course of action or events.

Sequin (1582), a small, shining metal or plastic disk or spangle used to decorate theatrical costumes and women's clothes, comes, via French **sequin,** from Italian **zecchino,** the diminutive form of **zecca,** "mint" (and originally from Arabic **sikkah,** "coin, die for coining"). The word has been applied to a former gold coin of Venice, introduced in 1284; to a former gold coin of Turkey, introduced in 1478; and to a former gold coin of Malta, introduced around 1535. It was not until the late nineteenth century that **sequin** was used to denote a shining spangle on clothing.

S**oda** (1558), from Italian **soda** "soda, barilla plant" (perhaps from Arabic **suwwadah,** the name of a plant), is a drink made with soda water, flavoring, ice cream, and milk; or a carbonated beverage; or a shortened form of **sodium hydroxide, sodium monoxide, sodium carbonate,** or **sodium bicarbonate.** In the sixteenth and seventeenth centuries, **soda** was used in English as a synonym for **headache.**

S**onata** (1694), from Italian **sonata,** "having been sounded, sound-piece" (formed from the verb **sonare,** "to sound"), is an instrumental piece of music in several (usually three or four) movements, often in different keys. Sonatas are written for piano or for violin, cello, flute, oboe, and so on, with piano accompaniment. Mozart, Beethoven (who wrote the famous *Moonlight* Sonata), G. B. Sammartini, Haydn, Schubert, Schumann, Chopin, Lizst, and Brahms all contributed to the sonata genre.

S**paghetti** (1888), pasta made in the form of long strings, boiled, and served with various sauces, comes from Italian **spaghetti,** the plural of **spaghetto,** "a little thin rope," the diminutive of **spago,** "thin rope." **Spaghettini** (1923) is a pasta thinner than spaghetti but thicker than vermicelli. **Spaghetti strap** is the name of a thin, cordlike shoulder strap on a bare-shouldered woman's garment. In the early 1970s, the term **spaghetti western** became popular. At first a dismissive name for the blood-bespattered imitations of American westerns produced by Italians in the 1960s, the term eventually lost all of its negative connotations. Shot in Italy (outside Rome) and Spain (outside Almeria), spaghetti westerns generally used Italian actors and American stars, such as Clint Eastwood and Lee Van Cleef. Quintessential examples of the genre include *A Fistful of Dollars; For a Few Dollars More; The Good, the Bad, and the Ugly; Once Upon a Time in the West;* and *Sabata.* The Japanese equivalent of a spaghetti western is called, appropriately enough, a **sukiyaki western.**

Squadron (1562), from Italian **squadrone,** "big square," the augmentative form of **squadra,** "square," is a detachment of warships (a subdivision of a naval fleet) or of men. A squadron in the cavalry (a unit higher than a troop and lower than a regiment) consisted of between one hundred and two hundred men. In the U.S. Air Force, a squadron is the basic administrative and tactical unit (higher than a flight and lower than a group).

Staccato (1724), from Italian **staccato,** "disconnected," the participle of the verb **staccare,** "to detach," is used to describe a manner of performing musical phrases with abrupt breaks between successive notes.

Stanza (1588), from Italian **stanza,** "room, standing, station, stopping place," is an arrangement of lines of verse (usually not fewer than four), often having a fixed length, meter, and rhyme sequence. One of the earliest occurrences of the word in English is in Shakespeare's *Love's Labour's Lost,* when Holofernes says, "Let me hear a staff, a stanze, a verse; *lege domine.*" In Italy, the word signifies an apartment, chamber, or room. In the plural, it is applied to certain rooms in the Vatican.

Stiletto (1611), from Italian **stiletto,** "little dagger," the diminutive of **stilo,** "dagger," which is derived, in turn, from Latin **stilus,** "pointed writing instrument, stake," is a short dagger with a blade thick in proportion to its width or a small pointed instrument for making eyelet or embroidery holes. Stiletto beards, or pointed beards, were very fashionable in England in the seventeenth century. In the 1950s, very narrow, high heels on women's shoes, called stiletto heels, were extremely popular.

Stucco (1598), from Italian **stucco,** "plaster, putty, stucco," is a fine plaster, especially one composed of gypsum and pulverized marble, used in the decoration of interior walls, as, for example, for moldings and cornices. It is also an exterior finish for masonry composed of portland cement, sand, and lime mixed with water.

Studio (1810), from Italian **studio,** "study" (ultimately derived from Latin **studium,** "zeal, eagerness, devotion"), is the workroom of a painter, sculptor, or photographer. It is also a place for instruction in one of the performing arts (for example, a dance studio), a room from which news items are broadcast live or recorded for subsequent transmission (as a broadcasting studio), or the buildings and adjacent land used by a company engaged in producing motion pictures (such as a Hollywood studio).

tempera (1832), from Italian **tempera,** which is short for **pingere a tempera,** "painting in temper," formed from the verb **temperare,** "to mingle, to temper, to divide properly," is a technique of painting in which an emulsion consisting of water and egg yolk (or oil and egg yolk) is used as a binder. Tempera is applied in thin films or glazes, which dry instantly and become brittle. Hence, they are used on rigid panels of wood or Masonite covered with several thin layers of gesso, rather than on flexible canvas. The Egyptian portrait panels from the Faiyum in Roman times were done in tempera. Tempera was also used by Giotto, Fra Angelico, and Botticelli. In the twentieth century, American painters Ben Shahn and Andrew Wyeth especially have experimented with tempera.

tempo (1724), from Italian **tempo,** "time," is the proper speed and rhythm of a dance or activity, as well as the rate of speed of a musical piece or passage indicated by such terms as adagio, allegro, and largo or by exact metronome settings. In chess, **tempo** refers to the time or effectiveness gained or lost by a player in the number of moves necessary to develop a position or achieve some other strategic objective.

terra-cotta (1722), from Italian **terra cotta,** "cooked earth," is a hard, fired brownish orange clay, used to make decorative tiles and bricks, sculptures, pottery, and architectural ornaments. Terra-cotta is also a brownish orange color. Terra-cotta has been made throughout the world since Neolithic times. Among the finest early achievements in terra-cotta are the glazed Chinese tomb figures from the T'ang period, the Tanagra (Greece) votive figurines, the Etruscan sarcophagi and large-scale sculptures, and the Huari-style painted bowls of Peru.

torso (1722), from Italian **torso,** "stalk, trunk (of a statue), stump (of a cabbage), core (of an apple or pear)," refers to the trunk of the human body or to a sculptured form representing the trunk of a nude human figure (especially one lacking head and limbs). **Torso** is also used to indicate something that is mutilated or left unfinished, as a piece of writing. Alfred Hitchcock's 1954 film classic *Rear Window*, starring Grace Kelly and James Stewart, is undoubtedly the most suspenseful (and brilliant) motion picture ever made about a torso murder.

trampoline (1799), from Italian **trampolino,** "springboard," derived from **trampoli,** "stilts," is a sheet of elastic material, such as canvas, attached to a horizontal frame and used by acrobats and gymnasts as a springboard and landing area for tumbling exercises and displays. Primarily a circus attraction, trampolines became popular with both sexes as a form of physical exercise in the

United States after the U.S. Navy preflight program made use of trampolines during World War II to improve fliers' coordination and balance.

tutti frutti (1834), from Italian **tutti frutti,** "all the fruits," is a confection of mixed fruits, usually candied and chopped, used to flavor ice cream. Tutti frutti is also a synthetic flavoring that supposedly combines the flavors of different fruits.

Vendetta (1855), from Italian **vendetta,** "revenge" (derived from Latin **vindicta,** "vengeance"), is a family blood feud, frequently hereditary, in which the members of the family of a murdered person try to avenge the death by killing the murderer or one of his relatives. These prolonged feuds were customary among the inhabitants of Corsica and other parts of Italy, but the savage feud that existed between the Hatfields and the McCoys in the mountainous West Virginia–Kentucky border area in the 1880s clearly indicates that vendettas are not limited to Italy.

Villa (1611), from Italian **villa** (derived from Latin **villa,** "a country house, farm"), is a country estate, a mansion, or any imposing rural or suburban residence maintained as a retreat by a person of some position and wealth. One could include among the most famous villas in history those of Cicero and Pliny, Tiberius's villa on the island of Capri, Cardinal Richelieu's villa at Ruell, the Villa d'Este near Tivoli, and Palladio's Villa Rotunda in Vicenza.

Violin (1579), from Italian **violino,** "little viola," is the treble instrument of the family of modern bowed stringed instruments. It has four strings tuned at intervals of a fifth and a fingerboard without frets. The earliest mention of **violin** in English occurs in Edmund Spenser's *Shepherd's Calendar*: "I see Calliope speed her to the place, where my Goddesse shines: And after her the other Muses trace, with their Violines." The **violin spider** is a small orange-and-brown spider, found chiefly in South America, whose bite is deadly to man. The violin spider gets its name from the fact that its head is marked with the shape of a violin, the handle of which points toward the spider's abdomen. In 1979, hundreds of thousands of poisonous violin spiders, for whose poison there is no known antidote, invaded Johannesburg in South Africa.

Vista (1657), from Italian **vista,** "a view," is a distant view, especially one seen through a long, narrow avenue or passage. It is sometimes used figuratively of a mental view that has been formed over a period of time or a series of events.

Volcano (fifteenth century) comes from Italian **volcano,** which was derived either from Vulcanus, the ancient Roman god of fire and metallurgy, or from Vulcano, one of the Lipari Islands, north of Sicily, which was thought, in classical times, to be the entrance to the domain of the blacksmith god. A volcano is a mountain or hill with a cuplike crater at the top from which lava, steam, ashes, gases, and rocks are expelled. Numbered among the more spectacular volcanic eruptions are those of Mount Vesuvius in 79 A.D. (which completely engulfed the cities of Pompeii, Herculaneum, and Stabiae, wiping out about ten percent of the population of the three towns); Krakatoa, in the straits between Java and Sumatra, in 1883 (which caused a tsunami, or tidal wave, 120 feet high that drowned more than thirty-six thousand people); and Mount Pelée on the Caribbean island of Martinique in 1902 (whose incandescent avalanche killed the twenty-eight thousand inhabitants of the city of Saint-Pierre).

Zany (1588), an adjective meaning "ludicrously comical" or a noun signifying an eccentric person, a buffoon, or simply someone who plays the fool to amuse others, comes from Italian **zan(n)i,** the servant character in the commedia dell'arte. It is almost certain that Italian **Zanni** is the Upper Italian (Venetian and Lombardic) form of Tuscan **Gianni,** a nickname for **Giovanni,** "John."

So a zany is, literally, a John. The word first appears in English in Shakespeare's comedy *Love's Labour's Lost*, when Berowne says: "Some carry-tale, some please-man, some slight zany, Some mumble-news, some trencher-knight, some Dick, That smiles his cheek in years and knows the trick To make my lady laugh. . . . " **Zany** appears again in Shakespeare's *Twelfth Night*, when Malvolio replies to Olivia: "I protest, I take these wise men, that crow so at these set kind of fools, no better than the fools' zanies." The word also appears in the comedies of Ben Jonson, and in Alexander Pope's 1728 *Dunciad*: "Oh great Restorer of the good old Stage, Preacher at once, and Zany of thy age!"

Japanese

futon (1876), a thin quilt or mattress filled with layers of cotton batting and placed on the floor for use as a bed, is borrowed from Japanese **futon,** which is derived, in turn, from Chinese **pu-tuan,** "rush-mat seat."

hibachi (1863), from Japanese **hibachi,** "fire pot" (formed from **hi,** "fire," and **bachi,** the combination form of **hachi,** "bowl, pot"), is an earthenware pan or brazier in which charcoal is burned to warm the hands or heat a room. In the United States, hibachis are usually covered with a grill and used to cook outdoors.

kamikaze (1945), from Japanese **kamikaze,** "divine wind" (formed from **kami,** "god," and **kaze,** "wind"), is the name given to a member of a special corps of the Japanese air force during World War II who intentionally made suicidal dive-bombing attacks into enemy targets, especially American and Allied vessels. **Kamikaze** was also applied to the airplanes, usually loaded with explosives, used in such attacks. According to Japanese folklore, the word was first used to describe a supposedly divine wind that blew one night in August of 1281, completely destroying the navy of the invading Mongols. Kyushu samurai resisting the Meiji government in 1876 used the same word in calling themselves the League (**jinpuren**) of the Divine Wind (**kamikaze**). In recent years, **kamikaze** has become a popular word with American surfers, signifying a planned wipeout, taken, hands crossed over the chest, on the nose of the surfboard, with no hope of saving the board or avoiding the swim. And in Japan today, the word is used to describe reckless taxi drivers and skiers.

karate (1955) literally means "empty hand" in Japanese, from **kara,** "emptiness," and **te,** "hand." The Asian art of self-defense, in which an attacker is disabled by crippling hand and foot blows, originated in India. It was later brought to China by a Buddhist monk. In the early 1900s, Funakoshi Gichin, the "father of modern karate," introduced karate to Japan. Of the many styles of karate, the best-known Chinese style is **kung fu;** the most famous Korean karate is **tae kwon do.** In the United States, the United Karate Federation was founded in 1965.

ninja (c. 1980), a member of a feudal Japanese society of mercenary agents, trained in the martial arts and in stealth, who served as spy, saboteur, and, occasionally, assassin, comes from Japanese **ninja** (formed from **nin,** "endure," and **ja,** the combination form of **-sha,** "person"). A rash of low-budget ninja films were made in the early 1980s in the United States, but the popularity of ninjas took a strange turn with the appearance, several years later, of the Teenage Mutant Ninja Turtles, four crime-fighting, pizza-loving giant turtles who live in the sewers of New York and talk in surfer lingo.

tofu (1880), a soft, bland, white curd made in Japan and China from mashed soybeans, comes from Japanese **tofu** (which is equivalent to Chinese **dou,** "beans," and **fu,** "rotten, turned sour"), which is an allusion to how tofu is made. Tofu, low in carbohydrates, high in protein, and free of cholesterol, is made from curdled soybean milk.

tsunami (1904), an unusually large sea wave produced by an earthquake beneath the sea or volcanic eruption, comes from Japanese **tsunami,** "harbor wave" (formed from **tsu,** "harbor," and **nami,** "wave"). A tsunami is also called a **seismic sea wave** or, erroneously, a **tidal wave.** Tsunamis cross the ocean in the form of low waves at speeds up to six hundred miles per hour. Some waves have been over one hundred miles long. The most deadly tsunamis have struck Pacific shores. For example, in 1896, a disastrous tsunami's hundred-foot-high waves crashed onto the coast of Japan, killing 27,122 people. This occurred only thirteen years after a tremendous tsunami had wiped out countless villages in Java and Sumatra, killing 36,380 people after the eruption of a volcano on the island of Krakatoa. The American author Lafcadio Hearn (1850–1904), who was so enchanted by the physical and spiritual beauty of Japan that he spent the last fourteen years of his life there, provides one of the most chilling descriptions of a tsunami in his 1897 book *Gleanings in Buddha-Fields:* " 'Tsunami' shrieked the people; and then all shrieks and sounds and all power to hear sounds were annihilated by a nameless shock . . . as the colossal swell smote the shore with a weight that sent a shudder through the hills."

tycoon (1857), from Japanese **taikun,** "great lord" (derived from Chinese **da,** "great," and **jun,** "prince, ruler"), is the title used by the Japanese to foreigners when referring to the shogun of Japan. The word now signifies a businessman of exceptional wealth and importance, a powerful magnate. In the 1860s, it was commonly used in the United States with reference to Abraham Lincoln.

Malayo-Polynesian Languages

a **mok** or **amuck** (1663), from Malay **amuk (amoq),** "engaging furiously in battle, attacking with desperate resolution," is used in English with the verbs **go** and **run,** as in the expression **to run amok.** As an adjective and adverb, it means "to rush about wildly, murderously, or in a violently uncontrollable frenzy." It is also used of people who seem unable to restrain their impulses, emotions, or desires, and of epidemics and diseases that are out of control. The word was first used in English to refer to a frenzied Malay. In the seventeenth and eighteenth centuries, it was erroneously shortened to **muck.** For example, John Dryden, in his 1687 poem "The Hind and the Panther," wrote, "And runs an Indian muck at all he meets," and Lord Byron, in his 1824 poem "Don Juan," said, "Thy waiters running mucks at every bell." Captain James Cook, in his journal (of his voyages), defined **amok** as follows: "To run amock is to get drunk with opium . . . to sally forth from the house, kill the person or persons supposed to have injured the Amock, and any other person that attempts to impede his passage."

a **toll** (1625), a coral island consisting of a ring-shaped reef or a group of closely spaced coral islands, enclosing, completely or partially, a shallow lagoon, comes from **atolu,** the native name in the Divehi language of the Maldive islands for such a reef. It may be related to Malayalam **adal,** "enclosing, uniting." Charles Darwin's theory that atolls grew around volcanic islands that were submerged beneath the ocean surface is now generally accepted. About the only plants that grow on atolls are mangroves, coconut palms, and breadfruit trees.

b **amboo** (1598), any of various giant woody tropical and semi-tropical grasses, including some with hollow stems used for making furniture, receptacles, baskets, and utensils, and as a building material, comes from Malay **bambu,** "a large, hollow bamboo." The young shoots are eaten as a vegetable or are pickled and candied. Some species of bamboo grow to a height of 120 feet.

boondocks (1944), a remote rural area, back country, an isolated or wild region filled with dense brush, comes from Tagalog **bundok,** "mountain." An **s** was added, since English has the tendency to affix that letter to locations, as in **the sticks** (a synonym for **the boondocks**), **the damps,** and **the woods.** While the word means "mountain" to the people of the Philippines, American soldiers extended the meaning to any kind of rough country or out-of-the-way locale. Used by servicemen during World War II, the word **boondocks** first came to the attention of the American public during an investigation into the brutal methods of training used by the Marines at Camp Lejeune in North Carolina. According to the official records, young recruits were regularly subjected to forced night marches "into the boondocks" (of places like Paris Island), which included some low-lying swampy areas where at least one Marine recruit died. The investigation ended, but the word remained. Its infamous history all but forgotten, the word **boondocks** is now synonymous with any rural area distant from the excitement of big cities or large towns. By the 1950s, shoes suitable for rough outdoor use were regularly called **boondockers,** as can be seen from Leon Uris's adventure-packed novel of World War II Marines, *Battle Cry*: "Andy Hookans was dumping a can of footpowder into his boondockers." About the same time, **boonies** had become the slang equivalent of **the boondocks.**

caddy (1792), a small box, can, or chest used for keeping tea leaves, is borrowed from Malay **kati,** a weight used in China and the East Indies equal to slightly more than a pound avoirdupois. A tea **caddy** probably derived its name from the fact that the little box or chest that held the measure (approximately one and one-third pounds of tea) was confused with the measure itself. The caddy that carries tea leaves is in no way related to the caddy (or caddie) who carries clubs and balls for a golfer. The latter **caddy** is derived from French **cadet,** as in a military cadet.

Camphor (1313), derived from Malay **kapur,** "chalk, lime" via Arabic **kāfūr,** is a whitish, translucent, tough, volatile, pleasant-smelling crystalline compound obtained from the wood and bark of the camphor tree. Camphor is used primarily as a moth repellent; in the manufacture of celluloid; and in medicine as a liniment, a counterirritant for infections, and a mild antiseptic. It used to be taken internally as a heart and circulatory stimulant, and as an antidiarrhetic; it is no longer taken internally, since it is mildly toxic, and ingestion may produce harmful effects, especially in infants and children. It is also no longer used as an anti-aphrodisiac—something to counteract sexual desire.

Cassowary (1611), a large flightless bird of Australia, New Guinea, and the neighboring islands, related to the ostrich, is borrowed from Malay **kasuari.** Cassowaries often weigh as much as 140 pounds and are dangerous. Capable of killing even full-grown men, these sometimes pugnacious birds usually leap feet first on their adversaries and then attack with their claws. Their wings, completely useless for flight, are covered with stiff, featherless quills, like spines, which also serve as weapons. Females lay three to eight green eggs at a time, which the males incubate.

gingham (1615), a cotton or linen cloth, woven of dyed yarn, often striped or checked, comes, via Dutch **gingang,** from Malay **genggang,** meaning "with space between," hence, "striped" or "checkered." Because the colored lines of gingham are always on the grain, gingham fabrics have no right and wrong side in terms of color. Gingham was memorialized in "The Duel," one of the most popular poems written by Eugene Field (1850–1895) for children. It begins: "The gingham dog and the calico cat / Side by side on the table sat."

gong (c. 1600), a large disk-shaped percussion instrument, usually made of bronze or brass, that produces a deep, rich resonant tone when struck with a stick or hammer with a padded head, is borrowed from Malay **gong,** so named in imitation of the sound made by the instrument.

hula or **hula hula** (1825), a traditional Hawaiian dance characterized by rhythmic movement of the hips and symbolic and imitative hand gestures, is borrowed from Hawaiian **hula hula.** The hula is usually accompanied by drumming and chants, whose stories the dance is meant to illustrate. According to Hawaiian myth, Hi'iaka, the sister of Pele, the volcano goddess, gave the hula to the people of Hawaii. Initially, only authorized persons specially trained to hula were allowed to perform the dance in public. The hula is such an essential part of Hawaiian culture that it has its own patron deity, Laka.

junk (1555), a native sailing ship used primarily in Chinese waters, with square sails, a high poop, three masts, and usually a flat bottom, comes, via Portuguese **junco,** from Javanese **djong,** "ship, large vessel." Junks are quite seaworthy, as was shown in 1965, when one of them completed a nine-thousand-mile voyage from Hong Kong to Cannes, France. Although they are most often used for transporting cargo, junks have also been used as homes.

kahuna (1886), from Hawaiian **kahuna,** is a Hawaiian witch doctor, sorcerer, medicine man, or wise man. Since the 1960s, the term has been taken over by surfers to designate a "god" of surfing.

luau (1843), from Hawaiian **lu'au,** is a party or feast of Hawaiian food held outdoors and often accompanied by some kind of Hawaiian entertainment. **Luau** is also the name of a cooked dish of young taro leaves, served with coconut cream and chicken or octopus.

m**ako** (1727), a large cobalt blue mackerel shark of the At-lantic and Pacific oceans, comes from Maori **mako.** Con-sidered by many to be dangerous to man, the mako is one of the fastest sharks, piercing the water at speeds up to sixty miles an hour.

m**uumuu** (1923), a long, loose-fitting dress, usually brightly colored and garishly patterned, originally worn by Hawai-ian women, but now also worn as a housedress in some American households, is borrowed from Hawaiian **mu'umu'u,** "cut off," be-cause the yoke was originally omitted. The muumuu has a fasci-nating history. It was a local adaptation of the Mother Hubbard dress distributed by missionaries to the native women of Hawaii purportedly "to cover the glorious voluptuous bodies of the earth's most beautiful women" (O. Ruhen in *Tangaroa's Godchild,* 1962).

o**rangutan** (1691), borrowed from Malay **orangutan,** literally means "man of the forest," from **orang,** "man," and **utan,** "forest." The term was first recorded by a seventeenth-century Dutch physician named Bontius, who was stationed in the Dutch East Indies. The word, which today indicates a long-armed, largely herbivorous anthropoid ape of arboreal habits found in Borneo and Sumatra, was originally so imprecise that it misled the English writer E. Tyson in 1699 to identify the orangutan more with human beings than with simians. In the preface of his work *Orang-Outang, sive Homo sylvestris, or, The Anatomy of a Pygmie,* he wrote, "The Orang-Outang imitates a Man more than Apes and Monkeys do."

r**attan** (1660), from Malay **rōtan,** which may come from the word **raut,** "to scrape off, to pare, to trim," is the name given to various climbing palms found chiefly in the Asian tropics and subtropics (as, for example, in India, Sri Lanka, and Burma), and also in Africa and Australia. The tough stems of rattan have many uses: they are employed in making furniture, umbrella handles, and canes. They are also used in the manufacture of wickerwork, chair seats and backs, and baskets. Switches made of rattan have been used for striking people across the soles of their feet, as well as for beating the dust out of clothes. The earliest instance of the word in English, referring to a rattan walking stick, occurs in a diary entry of Samuel Pepys on September 13, 1660: "Mr. Hawley did give me a little black rattoon, painted and gilt."

Sarong (1834), from Malay **sarung** or **sarong** (ultimately derived from Sanskrit **sāranga**, "variegated"), is a loose-fitting skirtlike garment (the Malay national garment), which consists of a long strip of cloth, usually striped or brightly colored, worn around the lower part of the body by both sexes in the Malay archipelago and Pacific islands. Actress Dorothy Lamour was given the title "Hollywood's sarong girl" as a result of her role as a native girl in her first film, Paramount's 1936 *The Jungle Princess*.

taboo (1777), from Tongan **tapu** or Fijian **tabu,** "forbidden, prohibited," is used in English both as an adjective and as a noun. The adjective **tabu** means "banned by society as being improper or unacceptable (on the grounds of morality or taste)," "set apart as sacred," or "forbidden for general use because of supposedly supernatural powers." A person, a place, or an act can be taboo. The noun **taboo** signifies a prohibition against saying or doing (or touching) anything for fear of being punished by mysterious (or not so mysterious, in the case of societal taboos involving etiquette and morality) forces. The word was introduced into English by Capt. James Cook. When Captain Cook arrived in the South Pacific, it abounded in taboos. Ordinary people were forbidden to go near a tribal chieftain or any of his possessions, so awesome were his supposed powers. The forests in New Zealand were considered taboo. No hunting or lumbering could take place without a special dispensation. Pregnant women were restricted by a large number of food taboos, the breaking of which would lead to death or deformity of the offspring. Traces of food taboos can be found in myths and fairy tales from places other than the South Pacific, as, for example, in the Genesis account of Adam and Eve (and the apple), the Babylonian myth of Adapa, the Greek myth of Persephone and the pomegranate, the episodes involving the cattle of Helios and the provisions offered by Circe to Odysseus' men in the *Odyssey*, Snow White (and the apple), Hansel and Gretel (nibbling at the witch's candy house), and even Lewis Carroll's *Alice in Wonderland*. Sigmund Freud devoted much of his psychic energy to investigating incest taboos.

tattoo (1769), from Marquesan **tatu** or Tahitian **tatau,** "a mark," is the act or practice of marking the skin with permanent designs or patterns by puncturing it and inserting pigments. Tattoo is also the word used to signify the pattern, design, or picture on the skin. Marquesan islanders used to tattoo their entire bodies with elaborate abstract designs. Anthropologists are divided into those who assert that tattoos are primarily decorative, those who believe that they are an indication of tribal status, and those who maintain they are largely apotropaic, a means of obtaining magical protection from evil spirits. Examples of all three uses can be found. Some South American tribes tattoo images of arrows and teeth in the hope that representations of sharp objects will scare off evil spirits. In different cultures, different designs are said to cure illness, to increase the wearer's agility, to protect against snakebites, or to indicate that the tattooed person is of marriageable age or has taken an enemy's head in battle.

ukulele (1896), a small, four-stringed musical instrument, similar to a guitar, popularized in Hawaii in the 1880s, comes from Hawaiian **ukulele,** "leaping flea" (formed from **uku,** "flea, insect," and **lele,** "to jump, to leap"). Contrary to popular belief, the ukulele is not a native Hawaiian instrument, but is an adaptation of a machete, an instrument introduced into Polynesia by Portuguese sailors around 1880. The word **ukulele** started out as the nickname of a British army officer named Edward Purvis, who popularized the instrument at the court of King Kalakaua (1836–1891). **Ukulele,** "leaping flea," was a reference to Purvis's small build and animated playing style. After a while, the Hawaiians began to call the instrument a ukulele.

Mexican and Central and South American Languages (via Spanish)

a balone (1850), a large mollusk with a soft body and bowllike shell, comes from California Spanish **abulones,** the plural of **abulon,** which, in turn, comes from Rumsen, a Costanoan language formerly spoken in Monterey, California. The fleshy parts of the abalone are used for food, especially in California and the Far East. Although the outer surface of the abalone shell is rough and dull, the interior is used as a source of mother-of-pearl. An abalone is also called an **earshell** or a **sea ear.**

a vocado (1697), the pulpy edible fruit of various tropical American trees, also called an **alligator pear,** comes via Spanish from the Nahuatl word **ahuacatl,** meaning "testicle," no doubt because of the similarity in shape between the avocado and the male genital gland. The avocado was once celebrated in a didactic poem entitled "The Sugar-cane, a Poem," written in 1764 by an obscure eighteenth-century English poet, James Grainger: "And thou green avocato, charm of sense, Thy ripened marrow liberally bestow'st." Of Grainger's poetic endeavor, an unappreciative Dr. Samuel Johnson remarked to Boswell, "One might as well write 'The Parsley-bed, a Poem,' or 'The Cabbage-garden, a Poem.' " Interestingly enough, **avocado** is not the only word in English to be derived from the male genitalia. The word **orchid** comes from the Greek word signifying "testicle."

b arbecue (1690), an animal, such as a steer or chicken (or small pieces of the animal), roasted over an open fire or pit, comes, via Spanish **barbacoa,** from Arawak or Taino **barbacoa,** "raised frame of sticks." A barbecue is also the grill, spit, iron frame, or portable fireplace over which the meat and vegetables are cooked. Finally, the word **barbecue** is used of the social gathering, usually outdoors, at which barbecued food is eaten. There is a totally groundless etymology of the word from French **barbe à queue,** "beard to tail," supposedly an indication of the large percentage of the steer that is roasted.

barracuda (1678), from American Spanish **barracuda,** is a giant, torpedo-shaped carnivorous fish of the perch family, from six to ten feet in length, found in tropical and subtropical waters. Divers are generally more wary of barracudas than they are of sharks because the former follow divers menacingly and are known to make direct attacks on bathers. Their long jaws are lined with large, fanglike teeth that leave deep, clean wounds with no jagged edges. Barracudas are considered a tasty delicacy, even though their habit of feeding on puffers (which have poisonous body parts) has occasionally resulted in the tropical-fish poisoning of people who have eaten barracudas.

cannibal (1553), from Arawak **caribal** via Spanish **canibal,** is a person who eats human flesh, especially for ritualistic purposes, or an animal that eats its own kind. The Arawak word seems to have meant something like "strong men," but the Spanish word was an allusion to the fact that the Carib Indians of the West Indies, called Caribales and Canibales in early reports, ate human flesh. The earliest mention of the word in English (in 1553) occurs in an account of Christopher Columbus's arrival on the Islands of the Cannibals, which he called Dominica (because the landing took place on a Sunday). Half-cooked human flesh, left by the Caribs, was found by Columbus and his men on the island of Guadeloupe. Forty years later, in Shakespeare's *Henry VI, Part Three*, Queen Margaret cries out to the Yorkist murderers of her son Prince Edward, "Butchers and villains! bloody cannibals! How sweet a plant have you untimely cropp'd!" The extent of cannibalism among primitive peoples has been greatly exaggerated, but the reputation of South Pacific islanders as cannibals is well deserved. Cannibalism was regularly practiced in the Marquesas and on Easter Island, New Zealand, and Fiji. In South America, moreover, the Tupinamba of Brazil and Chibchan tribes of Colombia delighted in feasting on prisoners of war. **Caribe** (1868) signifies a piranha, a small South American freshwater fish that occasionally attacks humans and other large animals that enter the water. The caribe derives its name from its rapacious and bloodthirsty propensities, supposedly reminiscent of those of the cannibalistic Caribs of northern South America and the Lesser Antilles.

Canoe (1555), from Arawak **canoa** via Spanish, is a light, somewhat fragile open boat tapering to a point at both ends and usually propelled by paddles rather than oars. The first canoes used by West Indian aborigines were hollowed out of a single tree trunk. The dugout canoe was also used by South Sea islanders, the Maoris in New Zealand, the Kwakiutl Indians of Vancouver, and several African tribes. Other early canoes were light wooden shells covered with bark, skins, or canvas. The first canoe club in the United States was the New York Canoe Club, founded in New York City in 1870. It was dissolved ten years later, when the American Canoe Association was formed by twenty-five canoeists at Lake George, New York. Today, many canoes are made of aluminum and fiberglass.

Chicle (1889), a gumlike substance from the latex of the sapodilla tree used primarily in the United States to make chewing gum, comes, via Spanish, from Nahuatl **tzicli. Chiclets** is a trademark, the brand name of chewing gum made into tiny, rectangular sugarcoated lozenges.

Chocolate (1604), from Nahuatl **chocolatl,** "article of food made of equal parts of the seeds of cacao and those of the tree called **pochotl,**" via Spanish **chocolate,** is a preparation made from the seeds of cacao roasted, ground, sweetened, and flavored with vanilla. The word is also applied to a beverage made from dissolving such a preparation in milk or water, to a candy, and to syrup. The first American chocolate mill was built next to the Neponset River at Dorchester, Massachusetts, in 1765 and was operated by John Hannan. In 1780, Dr. James Baker purchased the mill and began the present Walter Baker and Co.

Cocoa (1577), a corruption of **cacao** from Nahuatl **cacuhuatl,** is the seed of the tree more correctly called **cacao.** It also signifies the powder produced by pulverizing the seeds and the hot beverage made from mixing the powder with hot milk or water.

Condor (1604), from Quechua **kuntur** via Spanish **condor,** is the name applied to two large New World vultures, the largest flying birds in the Western Hemisphere. The California condor, dark gray-brown with white underwings, is a nearly extinct vulture found in the mountains of southern California. The Andean condor, glossy black with a large dirty white area on its upper wing and a white downy ruff around its neck, is widely distributed in the mountains of western and southern South America. Both condors feed primarily on carrion, but the Andean condor, more aggressive, has been known to kill wounded or young animals.

Coyote (1834), from Nahuatl **coyotl** via Spanish **coyote,** is the name of a relatively small, buffy gray wolflike wild dog, also called the prairie or barking wolf, of the Pacific slope of North America. The coyote has a narrow muzzle, slight build, and large pointed ears. In Native American myths and legends, the coyote is regarded as a culture hero and trickster. In the nineteenth century, **coyote-diggings** was the term applied by miners to small shafts in California, which resembled the holes of the coyote. Also in the nineteenth century, **coyote** was a slang expression for a person who made money by smuggling Mexican nationals across the border into the United States.

dory (1709), from Miskito **dori,** "dugout," is a small boat with a narrow, flat bottom and high, flaring sides. It was used by fishermen. Nathaniel Hawthorne, in his 1837 *Twice Told Tales,* wrote: "I launched my dory, my little flat-bottomed skiff."

hammock (1555), from Taino (or possibly Carib) via Spanish **hamaca,** is a swinging or hanging bed or couch made of netting or canvas and suspended by cords to supports at each end. Hammocks were originally used by sailors on board ship and by natives on land in hot climates or seasons.

hurricane (1555), from Taino (or Carib) **hurakan** via Spanish **huracan,** is a violent tropical cyclonic storm of the western North Atlantic, having wind speeds of at least 73 miles per hour. Hurricanes are accompanied by torrential rains. Their western Pacific Ocean counterparts are called typhoons. Hurricanes have resulted in loss of lives and destruction of property. Among the more disastrous can be numbered the hurricane of 1893, ranging from the Caribbean up to South Carolina, killing about a thousand people; the hurricane of 1900 that wrecked Galveston, Texas, and killed about five thousand people; and the hurricane of 1928, which, ranging from the Windward Islands to Florida, killed about four thousand people (1,836 in Florida alone). Since the early 1950s, hurricanes have been named in the United States. Some of the more destructive have been Hurricanes Carol and Hazel (1954), Diane (1955), Audrey (1957), Donna (1960), Flora (1963, killing about six thousand people), Inez (1966), Camille (1969), Fifi (1974), David (1979), Allen (1980), and Hugo (1989).

iguana (1555), from Arawak **iwana** via Spanish **iguana,** is the name given to several large arboreal lizards native to Central and South America, popular as pets. The largest lizard in the New World is the common, or green, iguana, which often attains a length of over six feet. Despite their clumsiness, iguanas habitually climb trees and use the power in their tails, which they aim with considerable accuracy, as a whiplash against enemies.

mahogany (1671), a word of obscure origin, perhaps derived from some non-Carib language of the West Indies, signifies any of several trees indigenous to the tropical parts of America, as, for example, Mexico, Central America, and the West Indies, that yield a hard, fine-grained reddish brown wood used in the manufacture of furniture. The word also signifies a rich reddish brown.

maize (1555), borrowed from Taino **mahis** via Spanish **maiz,** is the common name for Indian corn, a tall cereal plant cultivated in many varieties, bearing edible seeds or kernels on large, elongated ears.

manatee (1555), from Carib **manattoui** via Spanish **manati** (but commonly associated with Latin **manatus,** "furnished with hands"), signifies any of several tropical plant-eating aquatic mammals with two flippers in front and a broad, rounded, spoon-shaped tail. The manatee inhabits the shallow waters of rivers and estuaries of the West Indies, Florida, and the Gulf Coast, surfacing every twelve to fifteen minutes to breathe. In captivity, an adult manatee eats fifty-five to sixty-five pounds of lettuce and other vegetables daily.

marijuana (1894), a tall, coarse hemp plant whose dried leaves, stems, and female flowers are used in cigarette form as an intoxicant or hallucinogen, comes from Mexican Spanish **marihuana,** which has been traditionally connected with the female personal name Maria Juana. The slang **Mary Jane** is a translation of the name. The flowering tops of the same female hemp plant also yield the concentrated resin called **hashish.**

maroon (1666), the verb meaning "to put ashore and abandon someone on a desolate island or coast usually without resources," is borrowed, via French **mar(r)on** from American Spanish **cimarron**, "wild, savage," which was first used to describe domestic animals that had escaped into the wild. It was later employed as a noun to signify fugitive black slaves of the seventeenth and eighteenth centuries, and their descendants, who were hiding out in the mountains and rough country of the West Indies and Dutch Guiana. By 1709, it was being used as a verb to mean "to be abandoned," especially in the sense of "to be abandoned as a punishment," as often happened to prisoners of roving buccaneers. The verb **maroon** is in no way related to the dark brownish red color **maroon**, which comes from French **marron**, "chestnut."

petunia (1825), a garden plant of the nightshade family with white, violet, or purple funnel-shaped flowers, comes, via obsolete French **petun**, "tobacco," from Tupi **petyn**, "tobacco," since the petunia is botanically related to the tobacco plant.

poncho (1717), from Araucanian **pontho**, "woolen fabric," via Spanish **poncho**, is a blanketlike cloak with a hole in the middle for the head. In May 1849, *The Illustrated London News* proclaimed ponchos fashionable: "One of the chief novelties of the season, suitable for promenading or for evening wear, is the Poncho." Today, it is usually a waterproof garment that resembles a cloth poncho and is worn as a raincoat.

potato (1555), from Taino via Spanish **patata**, is the edible starchy tuber of a cultivated plant of the nightshade family. Potatoes were first seen by the Spaniards in the early 1500s either in the West Indies or in northern Peru. Potatoes were introduced into Spain by 1570. By 1600, they were being grown throughout Europe as a garden novelty rather than as food, since many people, aware of their kinship to the poisonous nightshade, were afraid to eat them. To the first English who ate them, thinking they were to be eaten raw, potatoes had the taste of raw chestnuts. In the sixteenth and seventeenth centuries, potatoes were believed to possess aphrodisiac qualities. The potato chip, a thin slice of white potato fried until crisp and generally salted, is also called the **Saratoga chip,** since it was supposedly invented in 1853 by a Native American chef in Saratoga, N.Y.

quinine (1826), a white, bitter alkaloid that is obtained from cinchona bark and was once widely used to treat malaria, comes from Quechua **kina,** "bark," via Spanish **quina,** short for **quinaquina,** "cinchona." Quinine, along with lime and sweetener, is an ingredient in tonic water, which is used as a mixer, especially with gin.

Savannah or **savanna** (1555), the name for a treeless plain found in various parts of tropical America, is borrowed from Taino or Carib **zabana** via Spanish **zavana** (now **sabana**), "flat country." The word **savannah** has been extended to signify grassland regions with scattered trees and seasonal rainfall in Africa, South America, Australia, and southern Asia.

Stampede (1826), from American Spanish **estampida,** "a stamping, crash," which is derived, in turn, from the Spanish verb **estampar,** "to crash, to stamp," is the name given to a wild, frenzied rush or headlong flight of a herd of panic-stricken animals, especially cattle, horses, and elephants. The word is also used of any sudden or unreasoning flight or rush of people in a body, be it in a supermarket, in a toy store during the holidays, or at a political rally for a candidate who seems likely to win. A stampede is also an extended festival or celebration in Canada or the western United States combining a rodeo with exhibitions, contests, dancing, and other social events. The Calgary Stampede in Alberta, Canada, for example, was first held in 1912 and has continued annually since 1919.

tobacco (1565) is borrowed, via Spanish **tabaco** from Arawak or Guarani **taboca,** the name given by the Indians both to the tube or pipe through which they inhaled smoke and to the roll of dried leaves kindled at the end. When Columbus came to the New World, he saw the Indians using tobacco, a plant of the nightshade family, for smoking, snuffing, and chewing. By the middle of the sixteenth century, smoking was introduced into Spain and Portugal by sailors returning from the Americas. In 1565, Sir John Hawkins, the English naval hero, returned from Florida to England with tobacco. In 1585, Sir Richard Grenville, an English naval commander, and a year later, Captain Ralph Lane, a colonial administrator, were the first to introduce pipe smoking to England. Right from the start, tobacco had its critics: James I of England placed a punitive tax on tobacco. There is a tradition that Tobago ("tobacco"), an island in the West Indies off the northern coast of Venezuela, was so named by Columbus because it was shaped like the pipe through which the natives inhaled tobacco smoke.

tomato (1604), from Nahuatl **tomatl** via Spanish **tomata,** is a plant belonging to the nightshade family that bears a mildly acid, pulpy red or yellow fruit cultivated and commonly referred to as a vegetable. Called a **love-apple** in France, it was thought to possess aphrodisiac qualities. The tomato, native to tropical America, was introduced to Europe in the middle of the sixteenth century. Tomatoes were eaten in Italy as early as 1554 and were commonly grown in English and French gardens by the 1580s. Interestingly enough, tomatoes were not commonly eaten in the United States until about 1900.

North American Indian Languages

C aribou (1665), any of several large, North American and Siberian deer that have antlers in both sexes and are related to the reindeer, comes from Micmac **yalipu** (from **yalipi,** "shovel snow"), via Canadian French **caribou.** The caribou was called a "snow shoveler" because of its habit of scraping aside snow with its front hoofs when it is looking for food. Caribou are especially adapted to cold climates, journeying in herds of tens of thousands to the tundra in spring to breed.

C aucus (1763), a private meeting of party leaders belonging to the same political party or faction to elect candidates for office, to choose convention delegates, or to decide on policy, probably comes from Virginia Algonquian **caucawasu,** "adviser, one who urges or encourages." Because the word looks like Latin, there are those who maintain that it comes from Latin **caucus,** "drinking vessel," which, in turn, is derived from Greek **kaukos.** This is less likely. The word was apparently first used in the name of the Caucus Club of colonial Boston, founded slightly more than ten years before the American Revolution.

C hipmunk (1832), a small, striped ground squirrel found primarily in North America but also in Asia, was originally **chitmunk** and was borrowed from Ojibwa **atchitamon,** the name of a red squirrel. The Ojibwa word **atchitamon** is derived from **atchit-,** "headfirst, facedown," and was so called from the squirrel's method of descending trees.

h ickory (1653), any of several North American trees of the walnut family, certain species of which bear edible nuts or yield a tough, straight-grained, heavy wood, comes from Virginia

Algonquian **pawcohiccora,** the native American name for a milky drink prepared from hickory nuts. Hickory is used to make charcoal. Pignut hickory, so named during the colonial period, when hogs ate the nuts with gusto, is used to make skis and tool handles. American Indians extracted the oil from butternut hickory for use in religious ceremonies.

hominy (1629), whole kernels of corn that have been bleached in a lye bath, washed in order to remove the hulls and germ, and then ground more or less coarsely and prepared for food by being boiled with milk or water, comes from Virginia Algonquian **uskatahomen** or **usketchamun,** meaning something like "grain that is ground or beaten." Hominy grits, a staple in the American South, are ground hominy grains served with fish, ham, or sausage, or made into a breakfast cereal with raisins, butter, and brown sugar.

moccasin (1612), a heelless shoe made of soft leather or deerskin, comes from Virginia Algonquian and is related to Ojibwa **makisin,** Narragansett **mokussin,** and Micmac **mkusun,** "shoe." Moccasins, with their soles attached to a U-shaped tongue of leather over the instep, offer surprisingly good protection against dampness. The Indians used to decorate their moccasins with porcupine quills until beads were made available by the European settlers. **Moccasin** is short for **moccasin flower,** another name for the pink lady's slipper, and is the name given to various venomous snakes, especially the cottonmouth, that live in the swamps and lowlands of the southern United States.

moose (1603), the largest and strongest member of the deer family, is borrowed from Algonquian (Eastern Abenaki) **mos,** "he who cuts or trims smooth," an allusion to the moose's habit of stripping the lower branches and bark from trees when feeding. The moose, whose huge antlers sometimes weigh as much as forty-five pounds, inhabits the forests of Alaska, Canada, and the northern United States. It is related to the European elk. **Moose** is also the name given to a member of the Loyal Order of Moose, a secret fraternal society founded in Louisville, Kentucky, in 1888.

mugwump (1832), the term applied originally to a Republican who refused to support the nominee, James G. Blaine, in the presidential campaign of 1884, was a nineteenth-century slang term shortened from Natick **muggumquomp,** "war leader, swift man." In 1663, the word **mugquomp** was chosen by John Eliot as the closest equivalent to the English word "leader" when he translated the Bible for the Indians. But it was Charles Dana, the editor of the *New York Sun*, who first applied it to Republicans who voted for Grover Cleveland rather than Blaine, the party's candidate. Today, the word signifies a person who remains neutral or independent on a controversial issue, especially in politics, or a member of a political party who votes for the opposing party.

muskrat (1620), an aquatic North American rodent with a musky odor, comes, by folk etymology, from **musquash** (related to Western Abenaki **moskwas**), meaning "the one whose head bobs above the water" (formed from **mosk,** "bobbing above the surface of the water," and **exkwe,** "head"). The muskrat is valued for its thick, shiny brown fur, used for coats and hats, and for its musk, which is used in making perfume. The word **muskrat** sometimes refers to the animal's fur or pelt.

Opossum (1610), which comes from Virginia Algonquian **opassom** or **opussum,** "white animal," is the name given to any of various small, largely nocturnal and arboreal American marsupials with prehensile tails. The most familiar opossum is the common, or Virginia, opossum, which ranges from southern Canada to northern Argentina. It is omnivorous, eating insects, fruits, eggs, fresh and rotten meat, and garbage. Opossum hunting is still a very popular sport in the southern United States, especially during the fall and winter months. The animals are treed at night with the help of dogs and flashlights. When captured, the opossum feigns death so convincingly that it turns away many predators, which has given rise to the expression **playing possum,** meaning "to pretend to be asleep or dead."

pecan (1773), a tall hickory tree of the southern United States and Mexico, cultivated for its olive-shaped, smooth-shelled, finely flavored nuts, comes from Mississippi Valley French **pacane,** which was borrowed, in turn, from Illinois **pakani,** "nut that is cracked" (and is related to Creek **pakan,** Ojibwa **pagan,** and Abenaki **pagann**). The word **pecan** is also used of the nut of this tree. The pecan tree figures in American history. Thomas Jefferson planted pecans at Monticello and sent several to George Washington, who planted them at Mount Vernon, where they grew into large shade trees (and are today the oldest cultivated plants on the plantation). The pecan is, moreover, the state tree of Texas.

persimmon (1612), any of several trees of the ebony family with oblong leaves, bell-shaped flowers and astringent, plum-like fruits that are sweet and edible when ripe, is borrowed from Virginia Algonquian **pessemmins** (related to Cree **pasimi-nan**), the **min** element meaning "fruit" or "berry." Persimmon sapwood is used to make golf club heads. Shuttles made of persimmon are extremely durable and favored by textile industry manufacturers. Tea made from persimmons was once used as a gargle for sore throats and thrush, and as a treatment for warts. Persimmons grow in great abundance not only in the United States but in Japan and China. Persimmon trees are sometimes called **possum wood,** because opossums are addicted to their tasty fruit.

powwow (1624), a ceremony among North American Indians, especially one that was accompanied by feasting, dancing, and magic performed for victory in war, success in a hunt, or the curing of a disease, is borrowed from Narragansett **powwaw,** "priest." The Narragansett word is derived from Proto-Algonquian

pawewa, "he who dreams," that is, "one who derives his power from visions." Actually, the first time the word appears in English (in 1624), it was used to signify a medicine man or sorcerer. Today, **powwow** is applied not only to a conference with Indians but, informally, to any conference or meeting.

raccoon or **racoon** (1608), from Virginia Algonquian **aroughcun** or **arocoune,** "he scratches with his hands," is an American nocturnal carnivore with masklike black or dark brown markings on its face, a sharp snout, and a bushy, ringed tail. Although raccoons are omnivores and adapt well to the presence of suburban man and the ubiquitous garbage pail, they prefer aquatic food and are excellent fishers. When they find something, they inevitably handle it for a while before eating it, a habit that has given rise to the popular belief that raccoons are fastidious animals who wash their food before consuming it.

sachem (1622), the chief or supreme head of an Indian tribe or confederation, or the title given to members of the governing body of the League of the Iroquois, is derived from Algonquian **sachim** or Narragansett **sachima** (both of which are related to Micmac **sakumow,** Penobscot **sagamo,** and Abenaki **sagimau,** "he prevails over"). The English word **sagamore,** also signifying a chief or leader among the Indians of New England, is derived from the same Amerindian words. **Sachem** was used in the United States in the late 1800s as a slang term for a political party leader. Actually, **sachem** was first used by the members of Tammany Hall, the Democratic party organization in New York City that eventually became synonymous with political corruption and scandal. Founded in 1789 by William Mooney, the Society of St. Tammany had thirteen trustees (the number commemorating the thirteen original states), who were called sachems. The president of Tammany Hall was the grand sachem, and presidents of the United States were given the title of Great Grand Sachem. Andrew Jackson was the last president to receive such a title. At meetings, the master of ceremonies was a sagamore, and a meeting place was a wigwam. The most infamous sachem of Tammany Hall was William M. "Boss" Tweed, who gained almost complete control of the Democratic party in New York City. Tweed, together with his cronies, or the so-called Tweed Ring, swindled the taxpayers out of millions of dollars before he was arrested. He died in the Ludlow Street Jail in 1876.

Skunk (1634), from Algonquian **sekakwa** or **segankw,** "urinating fox" (formed from **sek-,** "urinate," and **akw,** "fox, foxlike animal"), is the name given to a small North American black-and-white mammal of the weasel family that ejects a foulsmelling anal secretion when alarmed or attacked. By means of forceful muscular contractions, the skunk can discharge the fetid spray as far as ten or fifteen feet away. The most common deodorant for skunk spray is tomato juice.

Squash (1643), from Natick and Narragansett **askutasquash** (formed from **asq,** "raw, uncooked"), is the fruit of any of various plants of the gourd family eaten as a vegetable. Squashes are believed to have originated in Chile or Peru, but several varieties of squash were in common use among North American Indians when the first colonists arrived from Europe. Two of the most popular summer squashes in the United States are the zucchini and the crookneck. The most familiar winter squashes include the buttercup and the acorn.

Succotash (1751), from Narragansett **msickquatash,** "boiled whole kernels of corn" (related to Abenaki **mesikoutar,** which may mean "fragments"), is a cooked dish of corn kernels and lima beans (and sometimes sweet peppers).

toboggan (1829), a long, light, flat-bottomed sled made of a thin, polished board curved at the front, often with low handrails on the sides, comes from Micmac **tobagan,** "instrument for dragging," via Canadian French. Toboggans were first used by the

Canadian Indians to carry supplies over the snow. Today, they are used primarily to coast down prepared snow- and ice-covered slopes. Tobogganing became popular as a sport when the first runs were constructed at resorts and country clubs toward the end of the nineteenth century.

Wigwam (1628), from Abenaki **wikewam,** "their house," or Ojibwa **wigwaum,** is an American Indian hut having a rounded or oval framework formed of poles overlaid with bark, rush mats, or hides. Wigwams were used by the Indians of the Great Lakes region and correspond to the tepees of other tribes. The Wigwam was another name for Tammany Hall in New York City, the headquarters of the Democratic political organization in New York. Tammany, by the way, was the name of a seventeenth-century Delaware Indian chief, who was later jokingly canonized as the patron saint of the United States.

Woodchuck (1674), from Narragansett **ockqutchaun** or Cree **otchock** or Ojibwa **otchig,** "fisher," also called a groundhog, is an extremely fat American burrowing rodent that hibernates in the winter. The **wood** and the **chuck** of the English word are probably the result of a reshaping by folk etymology of one of the aforementioned Algonquian words.

Persian and Turkish

bazaar (1599), from Persian **bāzār,** "market," is a Middle Eastern marketplace or shopping area, consisting of shops or stalls, where all kinds of merchandise are sold. Today, the word is also applied to a sale of articles, usually contributed, for charitable purposes.

b **osh** (1834), nonsense or foolish talk, is borrowed from Turkish **bos,** "empty, worthless." The word suddenly became popular when it appeared in one of the best-selling books of 1834, *Ayesha,* by a now obscure British novelist named James J. Morier (1780–1849).

C **aftan** (1591), a long-sleeved cotton or silk garment worn in the Middle East that is tied at the waist with a girdle and worn under a coat, comes from Persian **qaftān** via Turkish and Russian **kaftan.** The word is also used to indicate a full, loose-fitting robe with wide sleeves that is worn in Western countries at home for lounging or entertaining or at the beach to cover up one's bathing suit. Caftans were very fashionable in the United States and Europe in the late 1960s.

C **aravan** (1599), from Persian **kārwān,** "company of travelers," via Italian **caravana,** is a group of travelers, such as merchants or pilgrims, journeying together for the sake of safety through deserts, mountainous regions, inhospitable territory, and the like. Organized primarily, though not exclusively, for trade, caravans have varied in size from half a dozen members to thousands. Pack animals, especially the camel after the first century A.D., have often been used to carry baggage and passengers. The North American equivalent of the caravan was the wagon train, in which people traveled westward largely to settle. **Caravansary** or **caravanserai** (1599), an inn, usually a large quadrangular building with a spacious courtyard, to shelter travelers and to provide relays for official postal couriers, is borrowed from Persian **kārwānsarāy** (formed from **kārwān,** "caravan," and **sarāy,** "mansion, inn"). Besides providing overnight accommodations, caravansaries often sold fabrics, manufactured soap, or engaged in banking. Caravansaries were spaced about a day's journey apart and were occasionally fortified to protect travelers from bandits.

C **assock** (1550), a long, close-fitting garment worn by members of the clergy, choristers, sacristans, or others engaged in ecclesiastical functions, comes, via Middle French **casaque,** "long coat," from Persian **kazhāyand,** "padded jacket" (formed from **kaj,** "raw silk, silk floss," and **āyand,** "stuffed"). The ankle-length garment is usually associated with Roman Catholic and Anglican churches, although a lightweight, double-breasted jacket, worn under a Geneva gown (and also called a **cassock**), is used by Presbyterian ministers. Some linguists maintain that the word **cassock** is derived from a Turkic word that is the source of the word **Cossack,** the term applied to an elite corps of Slavic horsemen. According to this theory, the word, related to Polish **kozak** and Ukrainian **kozak,** was originally adopted as an ethnic name by Turkic tribal groups on the Eurasian steppes. The first use of the word **cassock** in English, in 1550, signifies a caped cassock worn by women. In 1574, it is applied to a long coat worn by soldiers. **Cassock** as an ecclestiastical garment first appears in 1663.

Caviar (1591), the roe, or eggs, of certain large fish, especially members of the sturgeon family, probably comes, via the obsolete Italian word **caviari,** from Turkish **havyar.** Caviar, whole or pressed and salted, is usually served as a gourmet hors d'oeuvre or appetizer. Most of the caviar eaten in the United States is from the Caspian Sea region. The largest eggs, which are removed from the fish's ovaries, are produced by the beluga, that is, the beluga sturgeon, not the whale. The word **caviar** appears in Shakespeare's *Hamlet* (1602). Hamlet says to the First Player: "I heard thee speak me a speech once—but it was never acted; or, if it was, not above once; for the play, I remember, pleased not the million; 'twas caviare to the general."

Checkmate (c. 1350), in the game of chess, the act of maneuvering an opponent's king into a check so that escape is impossible, thus concluding the game, comes, via Middle French **eschec mat** and Arabic, from Persian **shāh māt,** variously translated as "the king is nonplussed," "the king is dead," or "the king is left unable to escape." The name **chess,** by the way, is also derived from the Persian word **shah,** "king." The Arabs, who learned the game when they conquered the Persians in the seventh century A.D., introduced chess into Europe.

c **ummerbund** (1616), a broad sash worn at the waist, especially a horizontally pleated one worn with a tuxedo on formal occasions, such as a prom, wedding, banquet, or concert, is borrowed, via Hindi and Urdu **kamarband,** "loin band," from Persian **kamar band** (formed from **kamar,** "waist," and **band,** "band").

d **ivan** (1586), a sofa or couch, often without arms or back and designed to be used as a bed, or a long cushioned seat placed against a wall in Eastern countries, comes, via Turkish, from Persian **diwān,** "booklet, brochure." The evolution of **divan** from a booklet to a couch is fascinating. A divan was originally a little book, usually a collection of poems in Arabic or Persian written by a single poet. The word was eventually extended to other booklets, as well, such as tax registers, muster rolls, military pay books, and bank account books. It was not long before the word was applied to the buildings or offices in which these booklets were commonly used: **divan** signified a custom house, a council chamber, the privy council of the Ottoman Empire, or a smoking room. Finally, by 1702, the word **divan** was used to indicate the bench, usually long and cushioned, in the office, council chamber, or smoking room where one waited or engaged in business, as well as any plush sofa or couch in a private home. **Divan,** signifying a couch, is in no way related to **chicken** or **turkey divan,** the name given to a casserole of chicken or turkey breast sliced and baked with broccoli and hollandaise sauce. This edible divan is probably a representation in English spelling of the French word **divin,** meaning "divine."

d **olman** (1585), a long outer robe open in front worn by Turks or, more commonly today, a mantle with capelike appendages instead of sleeves worn by women, comes, via French **doliman,** from Turkish **dolama(n),** which was derived from the verb **dolamak**, "to wind around." Dolman sleeves are very wide at the armholes and taper at the wrists, usually cut in one piece with the bodice.

jackal (1603), a corruption of Turkish **chakāl**, which comes from Persian **shag(h)āl**, which is related to Sanskrit **srgāla**, "jackal," is the name given to any of several wild dogs about the size of a fox. Jackals, which inhabit Asia and Africa, hunt in packs at night with wailing cries and feed on small animals and carcasses. Because the jackal supposedly moves in before the lion and hunts up his prey for him, it has been called "the lion's provider." Jackals can be bred with domestic dogs, and the young from such a union are fertile. The word **jackal** is also used of people who act as accomplices or collaborators in the commission of base or dishonest deeds, or of people who perform menial or routine tasks for another.

jasmine (1562), from Persian **yāsman** or **yāsmin** via Arabic **yās(a)min**, is the common name for shrubs or vines of the olive family having fragrant white flowers from which a perfume is extracted. One of the most important forms is called **jessamine**, a variation on the word **jasmine**. Several other plants having similar fragrant flowers are called jasmine, even though they belong to entirely different families. The red jasmine is the source of frangipani perfume. The word **jasmine** also signifies a pale yellow color.

julep (c. 1400), a sweet drink consisting of syrup, flavoring, and water, is borrowed, via Arabic **julāb**, from Persian **gulāb**, "rose water" (formed from **gul**, "rose," and **āb**, "water"). In the United States, a mint julep is an alcoholic drink made with bourbon (or brandy or rum) and sugar poured over crushed ice, served in a tall, frosted glass, and garnished with sprigs of mint.

khaki (1857), a dull brownish yellow, a twilled cotton cloth of this color, or a garment, such as a military uniform, made of this cloth, comes, via Hindi and Urdu **khaki,** "dust-colored," from Persian **khākī,** "dusty" (formed from **khāk,** "dust").

kiosk (1625), a small structure with one or more sides open, used as a newsstand, telephone booth, or refreshment stand, especially in France and Belgium, comes, via French **kiosque** and Turkish **kiushk,** "villa, pavilion," from Persian **kushk,** "palace, villa, portico." **Kiosk** also signifies a summerhouse or open pavilion, often surrounded by a balustrade and found in gardens and parks in Europe. Sometimes the word is applied to columnlike structures on which notices, messages, and advertisements are posted.

mummy (1615), the dead body of a human being or animal embalmed by the ancient Egyptian method, comes via Arabic **mūmiyah,** "bitumen, mummy, embalmed body," from Persian **mūm,** "wax." The word is also used of dead bodies dried and preserved by nature, as, for example, frozen animal carcasses embedded in prehistoric ice. The name arose because the skin and bones of corpses embalmed by the Egyptians seemed to be blackened, an effect that the Arabs erroneously attributed to the use of bitumen in the embalming process. Persian **mūm** indicates that it was also believed that wax was used. No description of the embalming process survives in any Egyptian writings, but two Greek historians, Herodotus and Diodorus Siculus, have recorded what they were told about it. Preservation was achieved largely through desiccation, accomplished by the deliberate use by the Egyptians of dry natron (sodium carbonate) and by the natural drying effect of the hot sand in which the bodies were buried. After the soft internal parts of the body (the brain, lungs, stomach, and intestines) were removed, the cavities were filled with resin-soaked linen bandages, sawdust, or wood shavings. The body was then packed with natron, anointed with oil, and wrapped, limb by limb, joint by joint, in strips of linen. The process, from start to finish, took about ten weeks. The organs that had been removed, such as the brain, through a hole made behind the nostrils, and the intestines, through an incision on the left side, were placed in canopic jars. Mummification was practiced in Egypt until the fourth century A.D. The discovery of the tomb of King Tutankhamen in the 1920s and widespread stories about his curse aroused interest in the possibility of avenging mummies, which eventually led to the popularity of mummies in motion pictures. Among the more famous movies featuring mummies were 1932's classic *The Mummy*, starring Boris Karloff as a desiccated mummy in search of his dead princess love whose soul now resides in a young Englishwoman, *The Mummy's Hand* (1940), *The Mummy's Tomb* (1942), *The Mummy's Ghost* (1944), and *The Mummy's Curse* (1944), the last three all starring Lon Chaney, Jr. In 1959, Christopher Lee took over the title role in the first of three Hammer Studios mummy films—*The Mummy*—which was followed by *The Curse of the Mummy's Tomb* (1964) and *The Mummy's Shroud* (1967). The word **mummy** appears in English in 1400 as a medicinal liquid or gum of the substance of mummies; in Shakespeare's *Merry Wives of Windsor*, Falstaff uses the word to signify dead flesh: "I should have been a mountain of mummy."

Orange (c. 1350), a round edible citrus fruit or a color between red and yellow, comes, via Middle French **orenge** and Arabic **nāranj**, from Persian **nārang** (which may, in fact, be derived from Sanskrit **nāranga**). Oranges are among the world's oldest cultivated fruits. The sweet orange is thought to have originated in China; the mandarin orange, in China and Indochina; the bitter orange, in India. Indeed, India may be the native country of the orange, since wild varieties are still found along its northern frontier.

Paradise (c. 1000), borrowed from ancient Persian (Avestan) **pairi-daeza**, "park, enclosure" (formed from **pairi**, "around," and **diz**, "to mold, to form") via ancient Greek **paradeisos**, "park, pleasure ground," is another name for heaven, the Garden of Eden, an intermediate place where the departed souls of the righteous await resurrection, or any place (or state) of bliss, delight, or supreme happiness. Although Dante equated paradise with heaven in the *Paradiso* of his *Divine Comedy,* some Christian writers identify paradise with purgatory as the intermediate step in which the soul is cleansed before entering heaven. In Islam, paradise is heaven, a realm of incomparable sexual delights.

percale (1621), a smooth-finished, closely woven cotton fabric frequently used for bed sheets and clothing, comes from Persian **pargālah,** meaning "rag." Percale was first imported from the East Indies in the seventeenth and eighteenth centuries.

Scarlet (c. 1250), possibly derived from Arabic and Persian **saqalat,** the name given to a rich cloth, is a bright red color or cloth or clothes of this color.

Seersucker (1722), from Hindi **sīrsakar,** a corruption of Persian **shīr o shakar,** "milk and sugar," is a plain-woven fabric of linen, cotton, or rayon usually striped with a slightly crimped, crinkled, or puckered surface. The puckered effect is produced by slack-tension weaving. Half of the warp yarn is held under normal tension during the weaving, while the other half is kept slack.

Shawl (1662), a square, oblong, or triangular piece of material used as a covering for the head and shoulders, often in place of a hat and coat outdoors, is borrowed from Persian **shāl.** Shawls have been around for a long time: they were worn by men and women in ancient Egypt and Mesopotamia. Different varieties of shawls, in wool, silk, and lace, have been worn by the Greeks and Romans, the Celts, the Persians, and the Chinese (especially during the Han dynasty), and in pre-Columbian America.

taffeta (1373), from Persian **tāftah,** "silken or linen cloth," which is a noun use of the participle of the verb **tāftan,** "to shine, to twist, to spin," is the name given to a usually smooth, crisp, and lustrous, plain-woven fabric of silk, linen, acetate, nylon, or rayon with a fine crosswise rib effect. Originally, taffeta was almost always silk. The rustling sound of taffeta whenever it is worn or touched is the result of weighting, a process in which a fabric is impregnated with metallic salts. Used as an adjective, the word **taffeta** indicates things that are florid, bombastic, fastidious, or over-dressed, as in Shakespeare's *Love's Labour's Lost*, when Berowne talks to Rosaline about "taffeta phrases, silken terms precise, three-piled hyperboles, spruce affectation, figures pedantical."

tulip (1578), a bulbous plant of the lily family having lance-shaped leaves and large, showy flowers shaped like bells, urns, and saucers, is borrowed from vulgar Turkish **tulbent** or **tul(i)band**, "turban," because of the supposed resemblance. Tulips were introduced into Europe (Vienna in 1554, Augsburg in 1561, Antwerp in 1562) from Turkey in the middle of the sixteenth century. From 1634 to 1637, tulipomania swept the Netherlands, and people were willing to pay enormous sums of money (more than five thousand dollars) for a single bulb. The tulip craze had such disastrous effects on the country's economy that the Dutch government enforced strict laws for the cultivation and sale of tulip bulbs. Today, the tulip is the national emblem of the Netherlands.

turban (1561), a headdress worn chiefly in Eastern nations, is borrowed from Turkish **tulbent**, which comes, in turn, from Persian **dulband**, "turban." The turban, which consists of a long piece of silk, cotton, or linen wound, twisted, or folded about a cap or directly around the head, is worn especially by Muslim men. Turbans, especially several close-fitting off-the-face varieties, have enjoyed great popularity, especially among women, at different periods in Europe and the United States.

yogurt (1625), from Turkish **yoghurt,** is a fermented, slightly sour semisolid food made from whole or skimmed cow's or goat's milk curdled by the action of cultures. Once eaten primarily in the Balkans, yogurt has become increasingly popular in Europe and the United States. It was not until the bacteriologist Elie Metchnikoff, winner of the 1908 Nobel Prize for physiology or medicine, concluded that yogurt arrests intestinal putrefaction and is beneficial to digestion, that yogurt was valued for anything other than its refreshing taste.

Portuguese (and Tupi)

Cashew (1703), a tropical American evergreen tree of the sumac family that oozes milky juice when injured and has leathery leaves, yellowish flowers, and small, edible, kidney-shaped nuts, comes, via Portuguese **caju,** a variation of **acaju,** from Tupi **acaju.** Cashew apples, upon which the cashew nuts sit, are fermented in Brazil into **caju** wine. Between the double shells of the cashew nut is a blackish, irritating oil called **cardol.** Like the oils of poison ivy, poison sumac, and poison oak, cardol can cause a rash. Hence, it is removed during the roasting process. In India, the oil of the cashew nut was used in homes to protect floors from the attack of white ants.

Cobra (1671), a highly venomous snake of the Eastern Hemisphere, comes from Portuguese **cobra,** which is short for **cobra de capello,** "snake with hood." When irritated, the cobra raises the forepart of its body like a candlestick and spreads its neck into a hood. Cobras are found in India (where they serve as the main prop of snake charmers), Burma, and Thailand. The king cobra of Southeast Asia is the largest of all venomous snakes, sometimes attaining a length of eighteen feet. The Egyptian cobra, found in Africa, was the sacred snake of the ancient Egyptians and was probably the "asp" that Cleopatra took to her breast to commit suicide. One of the more bizarre varieties of cobras is the spitting cobra, which sprays its venom at supposed aggressors, blinding them. If the eyes are not washed out immediately, the venom may cause permanent blindness.

dodo (1628), any of several awkward, flightless extinct birds related to pigeons but larger than turkeys that used to inhabit the islands of Mauritius, Réunion, and Rodrigues in the Indian Ocean west of Madagascar, comes from Portuguese **doudo**, "simpleton, fool," which is no doubt an allusion to the bird's awkward appearance. Round and fat, dodos weighed about fifty pounds and were the largest doves ever to have lived. In 1774, Oliver Goldsmith wrote in his *Natural History* or *A History of the Earth and Animated Nature*: "Three or four dodos are enough to dine a hundred men." The birds had small wings of no use for flight, and blue-gray plumage. Dodos were first seen by Portuguese sailors at the beginning of the sixteenth century (around 1507); within two hundred years, they were completely exterminated by human beings, especially the Portuguese and the Dutch (Mauritius having become a Dutch colony in 1644), and by the animals—dogs, cats, monkeys, and rats—that had come with them. The dodo proper was extinct by 1681; its cousins, the Réunion solitaire and the Rodrigues solitaire, by 1746 and 1790, respectively. All that remains of them today are a head and foot at Oxford; a foot in the British Museum; a head in Copenhagen; and skeletons in various museums in the United States, Mauritius, and Europe. **Dodo** is also a slang term for a really stupid person or for one who is hopelessly old-fashioned and behind the times.

flamingo (1565), any of various aquatic birds with long, slender legs and neck, webbed feet, a broad bill bent abruptly downward at the tip, and rosy white to bright scarlet plumage, comes from Portuguese **flamengo**, "Fleming" (which is related to Spanish **flamenco**), apparently a humorous name derived from stereotypical images of the Flemish as a ruddy-complexioned lot. The flamingo's thick, fleshy tongue is covered with spines and works like a piston, pumping three to four times a second, sucking in water and organic rich mud.

grouper (1697), any of several large, solitary sea basses inhabiting West Indian waters and the Gulf of Mexico, used extensively for food, is borrowed from Portuguese **garoupa.**

Groupers vary in length from a few inches to twelve feet. The largest species is the Queensland grouper, which often weighs as much as one thousand pounds. The smaller the grouper, the more brightly colored and intricately patterned. The sexuality of groupers is fascinating. Some groupers are hermaphroditic, producing functional eggs and sperm at the same time. In other species, the fish becomes sexually mature as a female, but after several breeding seasons, changes into a functional male.

ipecac (1682), the dried rhizome and roots of a small creeping South American plant of the madder family, or a drug made from the roots, which is used as an emetic, purgative, and diaphoretic, comes from Portuguese **ipecacuanha,** which is borrowed, in turn, from Tupi-Guarani **ipekaaguene,** "low-lying plant causing vomiting" (formed from **ipeh,** "low," and **kaa,** "leaves," and **guene,** "vomit"). Ipecac is used to induce vomiting, especially when the patient has swallowed a poison. Smaller doses of ipecac loosen mucus and are used as expectorants in cough medicines.

jaguar (1604), a large, spotted carnivorous cat of tropical America, from Texas and New Mexico to Paraguay and northern Argentina, with a yellowish brown or buff coat with black rosettes, is borrowed, via Portuguese, from Tupi **yaguara** or **yaguar-ete,** originally a class name for all carnivorous cats, including the tiger and puma. The jaguar, somewhat larger than the leopard, is the largest carnivore of Latin America. It feeds on peccaries, capybaras, deer, tapirs, and crocodiles. The jaguar is incredibly strong and often drags large animals (like deer and horses) great distances over rough terrain in order to eat its victim undisturbed. Jaguars are excellent fishers, as well. It is said that jaguars move their tails over the surface of a stream or lake to lure fish within striking distance.

lingo (1660), possibly a corruption of **lingua (franca),** "(Frankish) language" through Provençal, Portuguese, or Polari **lingo,**

"language," signifies the language, speech, jargon, slang, or argot of a particular group or field. It sometimes simply indicates language that is strange or unintelligible to the person who labels it as lingo, as in this line from a 1660 issue of the *New Haven Col. Rec.:* "The plant [plaintiff] answered, that he was not acquainted with Dutch lingo." Thus, **lingo** has often been used as a contemptuous designation for foreign speech. Polari, incidentally, is a distinctive English idiom or argot in use since the seventeenth or eighteenth century among theatrical and circus performers and in certain homosexual communities. It is derived largely from Italian through **lingua franca,** the term applied to a pidgin, creole, or "mixed" language used habitually by people of different mother tongues.

m**andarin** (1589), from Portuguese **mandarim,** which is an alteration of Malay **mantri** (borrowed, via Hindi **mantri,** from Sanskrit **mantrin,** "counselor, councilor"), is another name for the standard Chinese language. **Mandarin** signifies, too, public officials in imperial China, of which there were nine grades, each distinguished by a different button worn on his cap. Mandarin is also a small, spiny orange tree native to China bearing fruit with thin, easily separable rind. It is probable that the mandarin tree was so named by the Portuguese because of the similarity in color of the tree's fruit to that of a mandarin's robes. Mandarin is, finally, sometimes synonymous with a pedantic official, a bureaucrat, or a person with great influence in an intellectual or literary circle.

m**olasses** (1582), a thick uncrystallized light to dark brown syrup drained from raw sugar or sorghum, was originally spelled **molassos** and has been borrowed from Portuguese **melacos,** the plural of **melaco,** which is derived from Latin **mellaceum,** "honeylike (wine), honeyed grape juice, must, new wine." Christopher Columbus encouraged the growing of sugarcane in the New World. By the eighteenth century, the molasses trade had become so lucrative in the colonies that it resulted in the infamous Molasses

Act of 1733, a British law placing a prohibitive tax on molasses, sugar, and rum, whose passage is usually considered one of the actions that eventually led to the American Revolution.

pagoda (1588), from Portuguese **pagode,** "temple," borrowed from Persian **butkadah,** "idol dwelling" (formed from **but,** "idol," and **kadah,** "dwelling, temple"), is a temple or sacred building in India, China, and the neighboring Asian countries, usually a pyramidal tower of several stories built over the relics of Buddha or a saint, erected as a shrine, tomb, or memorial. One of the most famous Chinese pagodas was the Porcelain Tower at Nanking, a nine-story structure whose brick walls were covered with subtly colored porcelain. It was destroyed in the 1850s. Perhaps the most impressive pagodas still standing are the Pagoda of the Six Harmonies, near Hangchow, China, which is thirteen stories (or 200 feet) high, and the bell-shaped Shwe Dagon Pagoda in Yangon, Myanmar, which is more than 350 feet high and completely covered in gold.

palaver (1735), from Portuguese **palavra,** "word, speech, talk" (derived from Latin **parabola,** "story, tale, word"), was first used, apparently, by Portuguese merchants on the coast of Africa to signify a talk or conversation with the natives. There, the word was picked up by English sailors and eventually passed from nautical slang into common usage. For example, in his 1748 novel *Roderick Random,* Tobias Smollett wrote: "Damne, said the outlaw, none of your palaver." Today, the word has several meanings. It signifies idle talk and chatter, flattery and cajolery, or a conference, as well as retaining its original (if seldom used) meaning—a long parley or discussion between people of different levels of sophistication or culture, especially between natives and Europeans (traders, explorers, or colonial officials).

piranha (1869), from Tupi via Portuguese, is a small South American freshwater fish that eats other fish and occasionally, when traveling in a large hungry school, attacks and inflicts dangerous wounds on humans and other large animals that enter the water. It is also called a **caribe** or **tiger fish.** The smell of blood attracts piranhas, and they have been known to reduce a victim to a skeleton in a few minutes. Despite countless stories (and several B movies) to the contrary, there is no documented proof of any human being's ever having been killed by attacking piranhas. Until the importation of piranhas was banned by federal law in 1961, they were sold in the United States as aquarium fish. Today the word **piranha** is used figuratively, as in this review from the *London Times* (March 14, 1977): "Gayle Hunnicutt turned Sarah Pocock into a deceptively girlish piranha who . . . planned to nibble into tiny pieces everyone in sight."

tapioca (1707), a food substance made from the fleshy roots of the cassava plant, used in breads and puddings and as a thickener in soups, comes, via Portuguese, from Tupi-Guarani **tipioca,** "squeezed out dregs" (formed from **tipi,** "residue, dregs," and **ok** or **og,** "to squeeze out"), the name given by the Tupi and Guarani Indians to cassava juice. Tapioca comes in granular, flake, pellet, and flour form.

toucan (1568), any of various strikingly colored birds of tropical America with enormous bills, comes, via French, from Portuguese **tucano,** which is borrowed, in turn, from Tupi **tucana** or Guarani **tucan.** Both the Tupi and the Guarani names were imitative of the toucan's varied calls, which include buglings; hoarse croaks; and sharp, shrill cries. The Toucan, Tucana, is also the name of a constellation in the Southern Hemisphere near the South Pole.

yam (1588), the edible starchy tuberous root of various climbing plants cultivated in tropical and subtropical countries for food, is borrowed from Portuguese **inhame** or Spanish **igname** or **(i)name.** In the United States, certain kinds of sweet potato are incorrectly identified as yams. The word **yam** may originally have come from Africa, since many of the West African languages contain a word resembling **yam**, as, for example, Wolof **nyam;** Fulani **nyami,** "to eat"; Twi **enam,** "flesh." Several dialects, moreover, such as Gullah, spoken by blacks in Florida, South Carolina, and Georgia, have similar words.

Zebra (1600), which is borrowed from Portuguese **zebra** or **zebro,** "wild ass," or Spanish **cebra** (perhaps derived from Latin **equiferus,** "wild horse"), signifies any of several African mammals related to the horse, each species having a conspicuous striped pattern of black or dark brown on white or buff. Zebras inhabit the open grassy areas in Africa south of the Sahara. They are immune to blood diseases carried by flies that are often fatal to horses.

Russian

babushka (1938), a woman's scarf or kerchief, usually folded diagonally and tied under the chin, is borrowed from Russian **babushka,** "grandmother," which is formed from **baba,** "old woman, peasant woman," and **ushka,** a diminutive suffix, since babushkas are often worn by grandmothers and peasant women in Russia.

beluga (1591), which is related to Russian **bel(yi),** "white," is the name given both to a white sturgeon found in the Black, Caspian, and Adriatic Seas and their tributary rivers and to the white whale, found in fairly large herds in the Arctic Ocean and in some northern rivers. The beluga sturgeon is an important source of caviar, isinglass, glue, and ladies' shoes. The beluga, or white, whale is actually a small dolphin that sometimes travels as far south as Japan in the East and Ireland in the West. These whales are also called **sea canaries** because of the various sounds—whistles and creaks—that they make.

mammoth (1706), a large extinct elephantlike mammal from the Pleistocene Epoch, is borrowed from Russian **mam(m)ot** (now **mamont**). The word was first used in reference to the remains of an animal found in Siberia. Indeed, mammoth remains are often found in the alluvial deposits of Siberia. Mammoths became extinct about three thousand or four thousand years ago. The best-known species is the woolly mammoth, which lived in arctic climates of North America and Eurasia. It had ridged molar teeth and a hairy coat. Frozen bodies of mammoths have been found in ice in both Asia and North America. The word **mammoth** is also an adjective signifying something that is immense or gigantic.

shaman (1698), from Tungusic **saman** via Russian **shaman,** is the name of a priest, among various northern tribes of Asia, who acts as an intermediary between the natural and supernatural worlds, using magic for the purpose of diagnosing illnesses and curing the sick, finding lost property, prophesying, and controlling events. The word has been extended to medicine men of other tribal peoples, such as the Dayak of Borneo, the northwestern American aborigines, and even to certain Japanese priests of Shinto and Buddhist sects. Often, the shaman goes into a trance state and is thought to be possessed by a spirit or minor divinity who speaks through him.

tundra (1841), from Lappish **tundar,** "hill," or Finnish via Russian **tundra,** is one of the vast, nearly level treeless regions of the arctic regions of Europe, Asia, and North America, resembling the steppes farther south. Tundra plants include lichens, mosses, grasslike herbs, and low shrubs. Animals found in tundra zones include the musk ox, polar bear, caribou, snowy owl, lemming, and ptarmigan.

Vodka (1802), a colorless liquor, originally made in Russia, distilled chiefly from rye, but also from barley, corn, sugar beets, or potatoes, is borrowed from Russian **vodka,** "little water," which is formed from **vod(a),** "water," and **ka,** a noun suffix. In Russia, vodka is customarily served in small glasses and then gulped, rather than sipped, as an accompaniment to hors d'oeuvres. In the United States, it is also used in various mixed drinks, such as a screwdriver (with orange juice), a Bloody Mary (with tomato juice), a sea breeze (with cranberry and grapefruit juices), and a White Russian (with coffee liqueur and milk or cream).

Scandinavian Languages

berserk (1818), meaning "frenzied" or "deranged," is often used in the phrase "to go berserk," that is, "to commit actions that are recklessly defiant" or "to lose oneself in a violent rage bordering on madness." The word comes from the **berserkr** of Norse legend, one of a group of ancient Scandinavian warriors who, in the heat of battle, fought with the ferocity of wild animals and were deemed to be invincible. The word **berserkr** itself is derived from Old Norse **bjorn,** "bear," and **serkr,** "shirt," and originated as the name of a mythic eighth-century hero who rejected the traditional protective coat of mail and wore instead a bearskin shirt. Berserk, the grandson of the eight-handed Starkader and the beauteous Alfhilde, had twelve sons, each as reckless and brave as their father.

geyser (1763), borrowed from Icelandic **Geysir,** the proper name of a particular hot spring in Iceland, meaning "gusher" (which is derived from the verb **geysa,** "to gush, to rush forth"), is a hot spring that periodically sends up jets of heated water and steam in fountainlike columns into the air. The word first appears in English referring to Geysir, the geyser in Iceland, but by 1780, it was extended to similar springs in other parts of the world. Old Faithful Geyser in Yellowstone National Park erupts once every sixty-five minutes, shooting water 100–175 feet into the air. New Zealand's Waimangu Geyser, which is now inactive, is on record as having sent forth jets of water and steam as high as 1,500 feet.

l emming (1607), a small, extremely prolific arctic rodent resembling a field mouse, comes from Norwegian **lemming** (which is related to Icelandic **laemingr**, "loon," and **la**, "to blame," and to Gothic **laian**, "to revile"). Lemmings are famous for their periodic migrations, through towns and across wet tundra to the sea, which occasionally result in mass drownings. According to one Scandinavian legend, seabound armies of lemmings, driven by an irresistible force, destroy crops, befoul wells, and contaminate the air, causing local inhabitants to suffer from jaundice and dizziness. According to another myth, lemmings are spontaneously generated from foul matter in the clouds and fall down to earth during storms. The earliest representation that we have of lemmings is a 1555 woodcut in *Historia de gentibus septentrionalibus* (History of the northern peoples) by Olaus Magnus, a Swedish Catholic priest, which alludes to both their origins in the sky and their bizarre, seemingly suicidal migratory behavior. Eskimos, too, believed that lemmings were not of this world: their word for one species literally means "creatures from outer space."

n ickel (1755), a hard, silvery white lustrous metallic element resistant to corrosion, used especially in alloys (as, for example, stainless steel) and electroplating, and as a catalyst, is borrowed from Swedish **nickel**, short for **kopparnickel** (from German **Kupfernickel**), meaning "copper demon," so called either because nickel, though it looked like copper, yielded none or because nickel, when heated, emitted toxic fumes, as if Old Nick, the devil, were around. **Nickel**, "demon, rascal, dwarf," is short for the proper name Nikolaus and is related to the **nickel** in pumpernickel bread and in Old Nick, which is another name for the devil. Nickel was isolated and named by Swedish mineralogist Axel F. von Cronstedt in 1754. Today, the word **nickel** also signifies a cupronickel coin (containing 25 percent nickel and 75 percent copper) used in the United States and Canada, which is one-twentieth of a dollar and equivalent to five cents. Nickel was used in alloys even before it was isolated. As far back as 235 B.C., the ancient Bactrians were minting cupronickel coins.

Ombudsman (1959), from Swedish **ombudsman,** "representative," (derived, ultimately, from Old Norse **umbothsmathr,** "commission man," which is formed from **umboth,** "commission," and **mathr,** "man"), is a government official (in countries such as Sweden or New Zealand) who listens to and investigates complaints by private citizens against public officials or governmental agencies. In 1809, the offices of **justitieombudsmannen** (abbreviated JO) and **militieombudsmannen** (MO) were instituted in Sweden. In 1968, these offices were replaced by four independent officers. The office of ombudsman was introduced in Finland in 1919, in Denmark in 1954, and in Norway in 1962. In Sweden, **ombudsman** is also the name of the representative of a trade union or business who handles the legal affairs and protects the interests of the group. In American universities, an ombudsman is appointed to resolve complaints between students and teachers or administration.

rutabaga (1799), from Swedish dialect **rotabagge** (formed from **rot,** "root," and **bagge,** "bag"), is an edible tuber related to the turnip with a smooth, thick, whitish or yellowish root. It is also known as a **Swedish turnip** or a **swede.**

Ski (c. 1755), from Norwegian **sk(j)i** (derived, in turn, from Old Norse **skith,** "stick of wood, snow shoe, ski"), is one of a pair of long, slender pieces of wood (or plastic or metal) fastened to the foot and used to glide over snow. Skiing, as a sport, can be divided into Alpine skiing, which consists of downhill and slalom racing, and Nordic skiing, which includes jumping and cross-country racing. Archaeologists have found primitive skis, dating back to 2000 B.C., in Scandinavian bogs. Skis were used in warfare as early as 1200 A.D. by the Norwegian army during the Battle of Oslo and, more recently, in both World Wars of the twentieth century. It was not until 1862, however, that the first official ski competition took place—near Oslo. Twenty years later, the first ski club in the United States was organized in Berlin, New Hampshire, just five years after the Christiana Ski Club, the world's first skiing organization, was formed in Norway. **Skijoring** (1910), from Norwegian **skikjøring** (formed from **ski**, "ski," and **kjøring**, "driving"), is a winter sport in which a skier is drawn over snow or ice by a horse or motorized vehicle. **Waterskiing** (1931), the sport of riding on skis while being towed by a speedboat, was introduced in the 1920s. There is considerable debate as to the actual inventor of waterskiing. Count Maximilian Pulaski maintained that he introduced the sport on the French Riviera in 1929, but Fred Waller appears to have skied on Long Island Sound five years earlier.

S lalom (1921), from Norwegian **slalom**, "sloping track" (formed from **sla(d)**, "sloping," and **lam**, "track"), is the name of a downhill race in which skiers describe a winding and zigzag course between artificial obstacles, such as flags, poles, or gates. The word now extends to any zigzag course, as, for example, those in which canoeists weave between obstacles in rapid water, automobiles are tested for maneuverability or drivers for their reaction times, water-skiers race quickly between buoys, or skateboarders weave in and out of barriers.

S morgasbord (1893), from Swedish **smorgasbord** (formed from **smorgas**, "open sandwich, slice of bread and butter," and **bord**, "table"), is a luncheon or supper buffet of different hot and cold open sandwiches, hors d'oeuvres, casseroles, smoked and pickled fishes, meats, cheeses, and salads. The word also indicates an extensive and heterogeneous array, any medley, miscellany, mixture, or mélange.

troll (1616), from Norwegian **troll,** "demon, giant" (related to Danish **trold**), is a supernatural being in Scandinavian folklore, originally a giant but later, especially in Sweden and Denmark, conceived as a dwarf, inhabiting caves, hills, and subterranean dwellings. Trolls are excellent craftsmen. Usually portrayed as malevolent toward humans, they sometimes steal goats and carry off children. They are said to eat men, porridge, and sausages indifferently. But even when hungry, trolls refuse offers of bread or other food from kindhearted human beings, because they can never harm anyone from whom they have accepted anything. The sight of the sun is supposedly fatal to trolls, causing them to burst into pieces. In J. R. R. Tolkien's *The Hobbit*, trolls turn to stone. Today, **troll** is sometimes used as a slang expression for a homeless person, especially one who lives or sleeps in the park or under a bridge.

tungsten (1796), borrowed from Swedish **tungsten,** "heavy stone" (formed from **tung,** "heavy," and **sten,** "stone"), is a rare, heavy, gray-white, ductile metallic element with the highest known melting point among the elements (3,410 degrees Centigrade). Found in scheelite, wolframite, and other minerals, it is used chiefly in filaments for incandescent electric lamps.

Spanish

alligator (1568), from Spanish **el lagarto,** "the lizard," (derived ultimately from Latin **lacertus** or **lacerta,** "lizard"), is either of two broad-snouted, egg-laying crocodilians with a special pocket in the upper jaw that receives the enlarged lower fourth tooth. The first American alligator farm was established in 1892 on Anastasia Island in Florida by George Reddington. **Alligator** is also a jazz term that signifies an enthusiastic fan of swing.

anchovy (1596), from Spanish or Portuguese **anchova,** is a small fish of the herring family common to the Mediterranean Sea. Anchovies are used as appetizers and garnishes, in salads, spreads, or sauces, or on pizzas. The word first appears in English in Shakespeare's *Henry IV, Part One*, as Pointz reads from a list: "Item, Anchovies and sack after supper, 2s. 6d."

armadillo (1577), borrowed from Spanish **armadillo**, "little armed (animal)," a diminutive of **armad(o)**, "armed, equipped with arms," is a burrowing, largely nocturnal mammal renowned for its jointed protective covering of bony plates and its habit of rolling itself, when captured, into an impregnable ball, sheltered by its armor. Armadillos reside in the warm parts of the Americas, from the southern United States to Argentina in South America. Perhaps the strangest thing about some armadillos is that they invariably have four young all of the same sex, all derived from a single ovum that, when it begins to divide, turns into four embryos.

balsa (1777), from Spanish **balsa**, "boat," is a tropical American tree of the silk-cotton family that yields an extraordinarily light wood that is used to make life preservers, rafts, floats, and model airplanes. **Balsa** is also used of any life raft made of balsa wood.

brocade (1563), a rich silk fabric woven with a raised overall pattern, originally in gold or silver, comes from Spanish **brocado**, "embossed" (which is derived, in turn, from Italian **broccato**, "embossed, studded," formed from the noun **brocco**, "small nail, stud, boss"). Brocade now includes any richly wrought or flowered fabric with an elaborate raised design. The earliest extant brocades come from China and date to the Sung dynasty (960–1279). The weaving of brocades was a major industry in Italy in the thirteenth and fourteenth centuries and was greatly influenced by imports from China.

bronco (1869), an untamed or imperfectly tamed horse, a range horse or mustang of California or New Mexico, comes, via Mexican Spanish **(potro) bronco,** "untamed (colt)," from Spanish **bronco,** "rough, rude, wild." The Spanish word **bronco** is derived from Latin **broccus,** "projecting," an adjective describing teeth. Since Italian **broccato** is also derived, ultimately, from Latin **broccus,** the California half-breed horse is etymologically related to the exquisitely woven brocades of China, Italy, France, and Spain.

cabana (1840), a lightweight structure resembling a cabin used as a bathhouse on a beach or by a swimming pool, is borrowed from Spanish **cabaña,** "hut," which comes, in turn, from medieval Latin **capanna,** first cited in the works of archbishop and author Isidore of Seville (c. 560–636).

cafeteria (1839), from American Spanish **cafeteria,** "coffee place" (formed from Spanish **cafe,** "coffee"), is a restaurant in which patrons serve themselves or are served at a counter and carry the food on trays to their own tables. A cafeteria is also a lunchroom or dining hall in a school, hospital, or factory, where food is dispensed from machines, served from counters, or brought from home to be eaten there. In 1925, the *Glasgow Herald* reported that "cafeterias, although a commonplace in America, are just beginning to have a hold in Paris."

canasta (1948), from Spanish **canasta,** "basket" (which is derived, in turn, from Latin **canistrum** and Greek **kanastron,** "wicker basket"), is a card game of Uruguayan origin similar to rummy and pinochle, in which the main object is to meld sets of seven or more cards. Canasta, which derives its name either from the unusually large number of cards in a meld or from the tray used to hold the undealt cards and the discards, is etymologically related to a canister, a small jar or box used in the kitchen to hold tea, coffee, sugar, or flour. Two regulation decks of cards with four jokers (a total of 108 cards) are used in the game of canasta.

Cargo (1657), from Spanish **cargo,** "load, charge," derived from the verb **cargar,** "to load" (which is ultimately borrowed from Latin **carricare,** "to load a wagon," formed from **carrus,** "wagon"), is the merchandise, goods, or freight carried by a ship, airplane, or vehicle.

Chinchilla (1604), from Spanish **chinchilla,** perhaps derived from Spanish **chinche,** "bug," because of the erroneous belief that the animal had a fetid smell, is a small South American rodent raised for its soft, pearly gray fur. The chinchilla, native to the mountains of Peru, Bolivia, and Chile, is now extensively bred in captivity. The first successful chinchilla farm in the United States was established in Los Angeles in the 1920s by Mathias F. Chapman, an American engineer, who imported fourteen pairs from Peru and Chile. The farm, later moved to Inglewood, California, eventually had more than 1,200 chinchillas. The word **chinchilla** now sometimes signifies a full-length coat or jacket made from chinchilla fur.

Chino (1943), a tough, twilled cotton cloth used for military uniforms and casual wear, is borrowed from American Spanish **chino,** "toasted," an allusion to the color of the cloth.

Cigar (1735), a somewhat cylindrical roll of tobacco cured for smoking and ordinarily wrapped in a tobacco leaf, is borrowed from Spanish **cigarro.** Some etymologists maintain that the word is a corruption of **cigarra,** "grasshopper, cicada," because the cigar has the shape of a paper cicada. The expression **close but no cigar,** indicating that an effort has been unsuccessful, is derived from the custom of giving cigars as prizes to winners. **Cigarillo** (1832), meaning "little cigar," is the name of a small, thin cigar or a cigarette wrapped in tobacco rather than paper. **Claro** (1891), from Spanish **claro,** "light," is the name of a light-color and usually mild cigar.

Cockroach (1624), from Spanish **cucaracha,** formed from **cuca,** "caterpillar," and assimilated by folk etymology to **cock** and **roach,** is the name of an order of primarily nocturnal insects with flattened bodies, many of which are regarded as domestic pests. Captain John Smith, whose rescue by the Indian maiden Pocahontas is legendary, provided, in his 1624 *Generall Historie of Virginia, New England and the Summer Isles,* the first description in English of the cockroach: "A certain India Bug, called by the Spaniards a Cacarootch, the which creeping into chests they eat and defile with their ill-sented dung."

Corral (1582), from Spanish **corral** (which comes, in turn, from Latin **currale,** "enclosure for carts," formed from **currus,** "wagon, cart"), is an enclosure for horses and cattle. It was also applied during the nineteenth century (when pioneers crossed the North American plain) to the circular enclosure formed by covered wagons used to defend an encampment against attack.

embargo (1602), borrowed from Spanish **embargo** (formed from the verb **embargar,** "to hinder, to arrest, to impede, to embarrass"), is an injunction issued by a government prohibiting the movement of ships into or out of the ports of a country. Sometimes, an embargo is issued to alleviate congestion due to insufficient facilities or to regulate trade. At other times, it is imposed for political reasons that occasionally lead to war.

escapade (1653), a daring adventure or reckless prank, especially one that runs counter to conventional conduct or undertaken to escape confinement, is borrowed, via French **escapade,** "act of escaping," from Spanish **escapada,** formed from the verb **escapar,** "to escape."

filibuster (1587), from Spanish **filibustero,** "freebooter" (which is ultimately derived from Dutch **vrijbuiter),** is an extremely long speech, sometimes lasting for days, or a series of irregular dilatory tactics by a member (or members) of a legislative assembly, especially the U.S. Senate, in order to thwart the will of the majority by prolonging debate and obstructing action. Among the more famous (or infamous) filibusters in American history are South Carolina Sen. Strom Thurmond's twenty-four-hour, eighteen-minute filibuster against the 1957 Civil Rights Act; Oregon Sen. Wayne Morse's 1953 filibuster, lasting twenty-two hours and twenty-six minutes, against the tidelands oil bill; and Louisiana Sen. Huey Long's rambling fifteen-and-a-half-hour filibuster, which included recipes for Southern "potlikker," turnip greens, and corn bread, against the extension of the National Industrial Recovery Act of 1935. **Filibuster** was first used in English (in 1587) to designate a freebooter or buccaneer in the Caribbean. In the 1850s, the word was used to signify adventurers and revolutionaries who, in violation of international law, took part in organized expeditions against Cuba, Mexico, and Central America to set up local governments that would apply to the United States for annexation. Two of the more notorious filibusters were Narciso Lopez of Venezuela, who attempted to free Cuba from Spain, and William Walker of Tennessee, who had himself elected "president" of Nicaragua. Both were eventually executed.

gringo (1849), a contemptuous name, in Latin America or Spain, for a foreigner, especially a citizen of the United States or Great Britain, is borrowed from Spanish **gringo,** "foreign language, foreigner," probably an alteration of **griego,** "Greek," which may be the Spanish equivalent of the expression "It's Greek to me." Since the word first appears in English in 1849, there is an ingenious theory, totally without substance, that **gringo** is derived from the first two words of the song "Green Grow the Lilacs," which was sung by American soldiers during the United States–Mexico War of 1846–1848.

guerrilla (1809), one who engages in irregular warfare, especially in hit-and-run tactics, harassing the enemy by surprise raids and sabotaging their operations, is borrowed from Spanish **guerrilla**, "little war," the diminutive of **guerra**, "war," originally a reference to the Spanish resistance fighters, the remnants of the defeated Spanish army, who, during the period 1808–1813, made brief, devastating attacks against Napoleon and his occupying forces. Even before the word **guerrilla** existed, similar tactics were employed by the Maccabees against the Syrians and by the American Francis Marion, the "Swamp Fox," against the British army during the American Revolution. More recently, Mexican irregulars fought successfully in 1847 against the army of Gen. Winfield Scott in the United States–Mexico War; Boer guerrillas capitalized on the weaknesses of the British in South Africa in 1898; T. E. Lawrence, "Lawrence of Arabia," led Arab irregulars against the Turks during World War I; and Ernesto (Che) Guevara perfected guerrilla operations (especially in urban areas) during the Castro revolution.

lariat (1835), a long rope with a noose of hemp or leather used to catch horses, cattle, or other livestock, or to picket horses or mules, is borrowed from Spanish **la reata**, "the retied (rope), the riata." A lariat is the same as a lasso. **Lasso** (1768) comes from Spanish **lazo** (derived from Latin **laqueus**, "noose, bond"). **Lasso cells**, a term coined in 1865 by the Swiss-American naturalist and Harvard professor Louis Agassiz (1807–1873), refers to the urticating cells of coelenterates (corals, jellyfishes, hydroids, and sea anemones), which eject coiled hollow stinging threads in the manner of a lasso.

macho (1928), from Spanish **macho,** "male, vigorous" (derived from Latin **masculus,** "male"), is an adjective usually applied to men with a strong or exaggerated sense of their virility, their strength, or their courage. This male pride is usually accompanied by the feeling that masculinity carries as a necessary concomitant the right to dominate. The noun **machismo** first appears in English in 1948.

manta (1697), from Spanish **manta,** "blanket," is a cloak or wrap worn in Spain and Spanish America, a horse blanket, and a tropical fish, also known as a manta ray or devilfish. Rays have flattened bodies and greatly enlarged pectoral fins attached to the sides of the head. Unlike other rays, manta rays do not live on the sea bottom. Mantas can grow up to twenty-three feet in width and sometimes weigh as much as one and a half tons. They give birth to only one offspring at a time, which can measure up to five feet. The delivery often takes place as the manta leaps out of water and then re-enters with a resounding slap.

mantilla (1717), a silk or lace scarf worn over a woman's head, often over a high comb, comes from Spanish **mantilla,** "little blanket," a diminutive form of **manta,** "blanket." The mantilla, popular in Spain and Mexico, falls over the back and shoulders.

mosquito (1583), a small, gnatlike insect, the females of which suck the blood of animals and humans, is borrowed from Spanish **mosquito,** "little fly," a diminutive form of **mosca,** "fly." Some species of mosquito transmit such diseases as malaria, dengue, and yellow fever.

palomino (1914), from American Spanish, a special use of Spanish **palomino,** "resembling a dove" (from Latin **palumbinus,** "dovelike," derived, in turn, from **palumbes,** "ring-dove," and ultimately from the verb **pallere,** "to be pale"), is a horse with a light brown, golden, or cream-color coat, pale, whitish mane and tail, and often white markings on the face and legs. The palomino is believed to have been developed, primarily in the southwestern United States, from Arab stock.

patio (1828), especially in the United States, signifies an area, often paved, adjoining a house and used for outdoor dining or recreation. The original meaning of **patio,** which is still widely used, as a courtyard or inner court, open to the sky, and enclosed by walls or low buildings, is borrowed from Spanish **patio,** "courtyard," literally, "open area," ultimately derived from the Latin verb **patere,** "to lie open."

picaresque (1810), from Spanish **picaresco,** "roguish, knavish," formed from **picaro,** "rogue, knave, vagabond," is an adjective applied to a style of narrative, originally developed in Spain, in which the adventures of an appealing rogue are described in a series of usually humorous or satiric episodes. Although the picaresque hero may be found in literature as early as Petronius's first-century novel *Satyricon,* the picaresque novel does not become a recognizable genre until the sixteenth century, with the anonymously written *La Vida de Lazarillo de Tormes.* Among the most popular picaresque novels can be numbered Alain Lesage's *Gil Blas* (1715), Henry Fielding's *Jonathan Wild* (1743), and, most recently, Saul Bellow's *The Adventures of Augie March* (1953). Perhaps the most engaging female protagonist of the picaresque novel is the eponymous heroine of Daniel Defoe's *Moll Flanders* (1722).

pinto (1865), from American Spanish **pinto,** "spotted" (derived ultimately from Latin **pinctus** or **pictus,** "painted"), is a horse marked with spots of white and other colors or an adjective meaning "piebald" or "mottled," used to describe such a horse. Pinto beans are a mottled variety of kidney beans widely grown in the southwestern United States and Central America. Barbecued spare ribs and pinto beans were a staple of the White House during the presidency of Lyndon B. Johnson. Pinto beans and pinto horses are etymologically related to such diverse words in English as **pinta** (a skin disease endemic to tropical America), **pigment, picture, depict,** and **pimiento,** all of them derived ultimately from the Latin verb **pingere,** "to paint."

platinum (1812), a soft, ductile, silver-white metallic element, unaffected by simple acids, very heavy, and malleable, used in jewelry, dental fillings, and chemical and scientific instruments, comes from New Latin **platinum,** which comes, in turn, from Spanish **platina,** "silverlike" (formed from **plata,** "silver"). Platinum, which was initially called **platina,** was discovered in Colombia in 1735 by a Spanish scientist named Antonio de Ulloa. Today, Canada, the Republic of South Africa, and Siberia produce almost all of the world's output of platinum.

plaza (1683), a public square or open space in a city or town, an area along an expressway where restrooms and service stations are found, the section of a highway where the tollbooths are located, a shopping center, is borrowed from Spanish **plaza,** which is derived from Latin **platea,** "street, open space," and, ultimately, from Greek **plateia,** "broad (way)."

ranch (1808), from Spanish **rancho,** "small farm, camp" (derived from Old Spanish **rancharse,** "to lodge, to be billeted"), is, most often, a cattle-breeding establishment chiefly in the western United States and Canada. It also signifies a large farm used primarily to raise one kind of animal (horses, sheep, beef cattle) or crop. A ranch house is a one-story house with a low-pitched roof similar to the houses originally found on ranches. The ranch house, sometimes called the California ranch house or the Texas ranch, was created during the Spanish Colonial period in the American Southwest in the 1830s. In the 1950s, the California ranch style, informal, straightforward, and easy to move around in (being close to the ground, without steps, and with a patio or porch for private outdoor living), reached the height of its popularity in the United States, since builders found the design easy to build and sell.

renegade (1583), borrowed from Spanish **renegado** (from Latin **renegatus,** the participle of the verb **renegare,** "to deny"), is a person who deserts a party, person, faith, or cause, usually in favor of another. The earliest occurrences of the word in English refer to apostates, to Christians who joined the Turks and became followers of Muhammad. Today, the word is also used of an individual who spurns conventional behavior.

rodeo (1834), a public exhibition of skills, most often a competition, that features traditional cowboy skills, such as bronco riding, steer wrestling, calf roping, and women's barrel racing, comes from Spanish **rodeo,** "a going round, a (cattle) ring," derived from the verb **rodear,** "to go around," which is derived, in turn, from **rueda,** "wheel" (from Latin **rota,** "wheel"). Rodeos are regularly held in the western United States, in Canada (which hosts the famous Calgary Stampede), and in Australia.

sarsaparilla (1577), any of various tropical plants of the lily family with prickly stems, small flowers, and a root that has been used to treat psoriasis and was once believed efficacious in the treatment of syphilis, comes from Spanish **zarzaparrilla,** "little bramble vine" (formed from **zarza,** "bramble, bush," and **parrilla,** "little vine," the diminutive of **parra,** "vine"). Today, sarsaparilla usually refers to a popular carbonated beverage, such as root beer, flavored with an extract or syrup made from the dried roots of the plant.

sassafras (1577), a small North American tree of the laurel family with egg-shaped leaves and yellowish green flowers, comes from Spanish **sasafras.** All parts of the tree are aromatic, the dried bark of its roots being used as medicine and, especially, as a flavoring agent. When the explorers of the New World first arrived, they were informed by the natives that sassafras would cure most illnesses. Consequently, there was a great demand in Europe for the new panacea. Not too long ago, the U.S. Food and Drug Administration banned the use and sale of a beverage made from an infusion of sassafras, called **sassafras tea,** in interstate commerce, because of its known carcinogenic qualities. Since high doses of oil of sassafras are toxic, it has also been removed from root beer. It is still used, however, to scent perfumes and soaps.

Siesta (1655), an afternoon or midday nap or rest, taken during the hottest part of the day in Spain and Latin America, comes from Spanish **siesta,** "sixth," which is derived, in turn, from Latin **sexta (hora),** "the sixth (hour)." The Romans began their day at sunrise, which was **prima hora,** "the first hour." They divided daylight, the time when the sun remained above the horizon, into twelve equal hours. Consequently, an hour in summer was much longer than a winter hour. The sixth hour was midday, which eventually became the time for an afternoon nap.

Silo (1835), from Spanish **silo,** "place for storing grain," is a structure, usually cylindrical and sealed to exclude air, in which fodder, such as corn and sorghum, and hay are stored. Silos were originally underground pits or chambers for the storage of fodder. The military use of the word **silo** retains the subterranean aspect of the original silo, since it signifies an underground installation, often made of concrete and steel, for housing guided missiles.

tornado (1556), a violent and destructive whirling wind that advances over the land in a narrow path, especially in the Middle West, accompanied by a long, funnel-shaped cloud extending toward the ground, is a modification of Spanish **tronada,** "thunderstorm," formed from the verb **tronar,** "to thunder," which is itself derived from Latin **tonare,** "to thunder." It is clear that **tor-**

nado was initially confused with the verb **tornar,** "to turn, to return," because of the turning, shifting, and whirling of the wind. **Tornado** is also applied to the violent squalls, with their torrential rains and sudden gusts of wind, that accompany thunderstorms during the summer on the Atlantic coast of Africa.

V amoose (1834), to leave in a hurry, to depart quickly, is a United States colloquialism that comes from Spanish **vamos,** "let's go," the first person plural imperative (or hortatory subjunctive) of the verb **ir,** "to go."

V anilla (1662), the aromatic extract obtained from the slender, podlike capsules (or beans) of tropical climbing American orchids, is borrowed from Spanish **vainilla,** "little pod, little sheath," the diminutive of **vaina,** "sheath," which is derived, in turn, from Latin **vagina,** "sheath." Used by the Indians of tropical America as a flavoring for chocolate, vanilla was introduced to Europe in the sixteenth century.

V igilante (1856), a person who takes the law into his or her own hands, often to avenge a crime, is borrowed from Spanish **vigilante,** "vigilant, watchful." Groups of self-appointed, law-enforcing vigilantes were organized during the California Gold Rush. The town of Dry Diggings was so notorious for its vigilantism, in fact, that it was renamed Hangtown. One of the most famous incidents involving vigilantes took place in 1851 in San Francisco. When it was clear that the city's law enforcement agencies were unable to control two gangs of outlaws, the Hounds and the Regulators, a band of vigilantes, led by Sam Brannan, seized and executed a well-known criminal named John Jenkins—an execution followed shortly by their sentencing several other suspects to death, deportation, or whipping. Five years later, when a newspaper editor was murdered, the vigilantes reorganized and executed James P. Casey, the murderer, and Charles Cora, another criminal.

In 1864, vigilantes in Montana executed Henry Plummer, a criminal who actually had had himself elected sheriff of the Bannack and Virginia City area so as to obtain information about gold shipments and pull off stage robberies with a gang of bandits.

Tibeto-Burmese Languages

Panda (c. 1824), from its native name in a Tibeto-Burmese language of Nepal, is either a bushy-tailed, raccoonlike animal, about the size of a cat, with reddish brown fur (and called the **lesser panda** or **cat bear**), or, more commonly, a heavily built, bearlike animal with striking black and white coloration (also called the **giant panda**) that lives in a few mountainous areas of southwestern China, subsisting chiefly on bamboo. The first Westerner to report seeing a giant panda, a French missionary named Armand David (in 1869), placed it among the bears. Later scientists classified it as a raccoon. Even today, there is little agreement. In 1937, the New York Zoological Park became the first Western zoo to have a panda. All attempts to breed giant pandas in captivity have been unsuccessful (the refusal of Chi-Chi, a female panda in the London Zoo, to mate with An-An, a male from the Moscow Zoo, being the world's most publicized failure) except at the Peking Zoo, which bred seven in 1975 alone. The giant panda is the emblem of the World Wildlife Fund, an international animal protection organization.

Polo (1872), a game, resembling hockey, played on horseback with long-handled mallets and a wooden ball, comes from Balti **polo**, "ball," which is related to Tibetan **pulu**. In polo, the two opposing teams composed of four players attempt to drive the wooden ball into each other's goal. Although the word **polo** is Tibeto-Burmese, the game originated in Persia (Iran) sometime before the second century A.D. Afterward, it spread to Tibet, China, and India, where it appealed to British cavalry officers. When they brought the game back with them to England, it gained great popularity there. James Gordon Bennett, the publisher of the New York *Herald*, introduced Americans to polo in 1876. Formerly an Olympic sport, polo was dropped from the agenda after the Olympic Games in Berlin in 1936.

yak (1795), a large ox with long, dark shaggy hair, a long tail, and long, curved horns, found wild and domesticated in Tibet and other high regions of central Asia, is borrowed from Tibetan **gyag** or **gyak.** The yak can live at heights up to twenty thousand feet and is the only pack animal able to work at that altitude. Its silky coat, highly prized by hunters, is made into rope and various fabrics. Its tail is used for decoration and, dyed red, as a flyflapper in India.

Yiddish

bagel (1932), a hard, leavened, doughnut-shaped roll with a glazed surface, is borrowed from Yiddish **beygel,** "ringlike thing, bracelet," because of its shape.

blintz(e) (1903), a thin wheat flour pancake, like a crepe, folded or rolled around a filling, usually of cheese or fruit, and then fried or baked, comes from Yiddish **blintse,** which is derived, in turn, from Russian **blinets,** "little pancake," the diminutive of **blin,** "pancake."

dreck (1922), a vulgar expression meaning "worthless trash," "rubbish," "dung," or "excrement," comes from Yiddish **drek,** related to German **Dreck,** "mud, filth, dung." The word first appears in English (in 1922) in James Joyce's *Ulysses:* "Farewell, Fare thee well. Dreck!"

kibitzer (1927), a person at a card game who looks at the players' cards over their shoulders and offers unwanted or gratuitous advice, is borrowed from Yiddish **kibetsn,** equivalent to German **kiebitzen,** "to look on at cards," which is derived, in turn, from **Kiebitz,** "busybody, lapwing, plover." The lapwing, a crested plover, is a bird that is known for its irregular flapping flight and for its shrill, wailing cry. A kibitzer also signifies a person who makes wisecracks or lousy jokes while other people are trying to finish a task or conduct a serious discussion.

klutz (1965), a slang term for a person who is clumsy, awkward, or socially inept, is borrowed from Yiddish **klots,** "wooden beam," which is related to German **Klotz,** "wooden block."

kvetch or kvetsch (1964), from Yiddish **kvetshn,** "to squeeze, to pinch," is used both as a noun ("a person who complains unremittingly or finds faults") and as a verb ("to complain a great deal"). The word began to appear in English in the 1960s, as, for example, in Saul Bellow's 1964 novel *Herzog:* "She's got a disgusting father and a kvetch of a mother." Or in Wallace Markfield's *To an Early Grave:* "There was Ozzie Waldman, Ozzie the kvetch. For his favor you could die. He gave away nothing."

maven (1965), an expert, one who is knowledgeable about a subject, is borrowed from Yiddish **mavyn,** which comes, in turn, from Hebrew **mabhin,** "connoisseur" (formed from **l'havin,** "to understand").

mensch (1953), from Yiddish **mentsh,** "person, man, human being" (related to German **Mensch,** "man"), is used informally of a decent, honest, upright individual, a person of integrity. In Saul Bellow's 1953 picaresque novel *The Adventures of*

Augie March, Grandma Lausch says to Augie, "I want you to be a mensch. You have less time to change than you think. The Klein boy is going to get you into trouble."

meshuggah or **meshuga** or **meshugge** (1892), from Yiddish **meshuge**, which is derived, in turn, from Hebrew **meshugga** (formed from the verb **shāgag**, "to go astray, to wander"), is a slang adjective meaning "crazy, foolish." **Meshugaas** (1907) signifies foolishness, nonsense, or insanity. **Meshug(g)ana** or **meshuggener** (1900) indicates a foolish or crazy person.

nebbish (1892), a slang term for a meek, luckless, ineffectual person, a nonentity, a nobody, is borrowed from Yiddish **nebekh**, "poor, unfortunate," used as an interjection. The Yiddish word may itself have been derived from a Slavic word, such as Czech **nebohy**, "poor."

nosh (1957), to snack between meals, to nibble, to munch, comes from Yiddish **nashn**, "to nibble, to gnaw," which is related to German **naschen**, "to nibble, to eat on the sly." Sometimes **nosh** refers to a snack bar or restaurant.

pastrami (1940), a smoked brisket of beef, cured in a highly seasoned mixture of sugar, peppercorns, garlic, and coriander seeds, comes from Yiddish **pastrame**, which is derived, in turn, from Romanian **pastrama**, "preserved (meat)," formed from the verb **pastra**, "to preserve."

Schlep(p) (1922), to haul, to lug, to move slowly or tediously, comes from Yiddish **shlepn**, "to carry, to drag, to trudge." The adjective **schleppy** means "run-down, sloppy, dowdy," as in a schleppy motel or a schleppy old housecoat. The word **schlepp** first appears in English in James Joyce's *Ulysses*: "She trudges, schlepps, trains, drags, trascines her load. A tide westering, moondrawn, in her wake."

Schlimazel (1948), a slang expression signifying an inept, bungling individual, one who is consistently unlucky, a born loser, comes from Yiddish **shlimmazl** (formed from **shlim,** "bad, crooked," and Hebrew **mazl,** "luck"). A schlimazel is similar, in many ways, to a schlemiel, an awkward or unlucky person. **Schlemiel** comes from Yiddish **shlemil,** which is borrowed from Hebrew **shelumiel,** a noun derived from Shelumiel, whose name appears both in the Bible (the Book of Numbers) and in the Talmud. In the Talmud, Shelumiel is said to have met an unhappy end. The use of **schlemiel** as an unlucky person who loses out in all his dealings was undoubtedly influenced by the adventures of the hero of Adelbert von Chamisso's 1814 prose tale *Peter Schlemihls wundersame Geschichte* (The Wonderful History of Peter Schlemihl), the story of a man who sells his shadow to the devil and lives to regret it.

Schlock (1915), used as an adjective meaning "cheap, shoddy" and as a noun signifying junk, something of low quality, comes from Yiddish **shlak,** "apoplectic stroke, blow, nuisance, curse" (derived from the verb **shlogn,** "to strike"). A schlockmeister is a person who purveys cheap merchandise and "special offers." The adjective **schlocky,** meaning "trashy," is also used in English.

Schmaltz or **schmalz** (1935), from Yiddish **shmalts,** "rendered fat, grease, lard," signifies exaggerated sentimentality, especially in music (violins and organs being especially schmaltzy) or drama (soap operas being the quintessence of schmaltz). **Schmaltz** is sometimes used to indicate fat or grease, especially melted chicken fat.

Schmear or **schmeer** (1961), from Yiddish **shmir**, "smear," and **shmirn**, "to smear, to grease, to flatter," is used variously of a dab or small amount (as, for example, a schmear of cream cheese on a bagel), a bribe, payola, flattery, or graft, and of an aggregate or number of related things, ideas, or plans (as in the phrase **the whole schmear**).

Schmo (1948), a slang term for a stupid person, an idiot or jerk, is probably derived from the vulgar Yiddish **shmok**, "penis," which is related to German **Schmuck**, "ornament, jewels, adornment." We are indebted to *Life* magazine (March 15, 1948) for the first attempt in English to define **schmo**: "Schlump is a friendlier, more sympathetic term than 'schmo,' which has completely replaced 'jerk.' A schmo, of course, is a person who stands watching a machine make doughnuts, and 1) cannot understand the process, 2) cannot get up will power to leave." In the 1940s, too, cartoonist Al Capp introduced into his hillbilly comic strip *L'il Abner* a race of endlessly proliferating creatures who resembled soft bowling balls and loved to be kicked—the Schmoos. **Schmuck** (1892), also derived from vulgar Yiddish **shmok**, "penis," signifies an obnoxious or objectionable person (or a jerk). In Bernard Malamud's 1971 novel *The Tenants*, a Jewish writer named Harry Lesser, talking to his friend, a black writer named Willie Spearmint, asserts, "Art is the glory and only a shmuck thinks otherwise." The origin of **schnook** (1948), another slang expression for a stupid person, a simpleton, a sucker, or a nonentity, is obscure, but the word may come from Yiddish **shnuk**, "snout."

Schmoose or **schmooze** (1897), used either as a verb meaning "to engage in idle conversation, to chat, to gossip" or as a noun signifying informal conversation or chatter, is borrowed from Yiddish **shmuesn**, "to talk, to converse, to chat" (related to **shmues**, "gossip"), derived, in turn, from Hebrew **shemu'oth**, "news, rumor, reports, gossip."

Schnorrer (1892), a slang expression for a person who continually borrows from others or who wheedles others into supplying his needs with no intentions of paying back, a layabout, a good-for-nothing, a scrounger, or a moocher, is borrowed from Yiddish **shnorer**, "beggar, sponger," which is related to **shnor(n)**, "to beg." The Yiddish word is related to Middle High German **snurren**, "to hum, to buzz, to whir," an allusion to European beggars' common practice of playing a small pipe or whistle (German **Schnurrpfeife**).

Schnozzle or **schnozzola** or **schnoz** (1930), a slang expression for a nose, especially one that is extraordinarily large, is borrowed from Yiddish **shnabl**, "beak," or is a modification of Yiddish **shnoitsl**, "little snout," the diminutive of **shnoits** "snout" (related to German **Schnauze**, "snout"). Or it may be a composite word formed from English **nose** and **nozzle**, the **schn-** having been added by association with various etymologically related Yiddish words. **Schnozzola** (or **"de Schnozz"**) was the nickname of American entertainer Jimmy Durante (1893–1980), whose unusually large nose was probably the most famous in the history of show business. Cole Porter included "the nose of the great Durante" together with Inferno's Dante, the Louvre Museum, a Shakespeare sonnet, a symphony by Strauss, Napoleon brandy, a Waldorf salad, Whistler's mama, and an O'Neill drama in his song "You're the Top," a catalog of people and objects that represent the ultimate in good taste.

Shtik or **shtick** (1959), from Yiddish **shtik**, "piece, pranks, whims" (related to German **Stück**, "piece, play"), is a slang term for an act or stage routine, usually comic, or for a gimmick or characteristic style designed to draw attention to oneself or to get a laugh. A film critic, commenting enthusiastically on Barbra Streisand's surprisingly restrained acting in the 1973 movie *The Way We Were*, said, "Minus the usual Streisand shtick, it is arguably the best performance of her career."

Yenta (1923), a slang expression for a woman who is a busy-body or blabbermouth, a meddler or a shrew, is borrowed from Yiddish **yente,** "vulgar woman," probably from the female personal name Yentl, which may itself be, ironically, a corruption of Italian **gentile,** meaning "kind, amiable, noble, highborn."

Zaftig (1937), from Yiddish **zaftik,** "juicy, succulent" (related to German **Saft,** "juice, sap"), is an adjective, applied only to women, meaning "curvaceous, pleasantly plump, having a full, rounded or comfortably ample figure." The adjective has been used, at various times, to describe such female performers as Gina Lollobrigida and Dolly Parton.